"We feel confused and even scared in these troubled times. A common tendency is to ignore our feelings and binge watch another series on TV or drink more martinis. Dr. Poonamallee offers hope in this marvelous book about meditation. She shows how kindness and curiosity are antidotes to self-centered self-righteousness that plague our lives. The practices and exercises she gently leads you into trying may offer more inner peace, harmony with others, and a sense of awe at the beauty in life and love of others."

Richard Boyatzis, PhD, *Distinguished University Professor, Case Western Reserve University, Co-author of the international best seller, "Primal Leadership" and the new "Helping People Change"*

"Dr. Poonamallee's work on leadership has been the single most valuable tool in my professional work in HR and organization development. For developing both established and new leaders in fast-moving technology companies, it's nothing short of revolutionary. Dr. Poonamallee's synthesis of mindfulness and emotional intelligence theories and practices as drivers of enhanced emotional intelligence unlock critical evolutions for a leader's mind. This level-up opens new possibilities for inspiring their teams, managing conflict and pressure, and building powerful new pathways to success for their businesses. As an invaluable bonus, these abilities prove incredibly powerful for self-actualization on a personal level."

Juliette Dupre, *VP – HR, Tik Tok*

"This is a valuable read for anyone attracted to ideas surrounding mindfulness, presence, self-reflection or meditation. And for those who are actively in searches for, 'Who am I?' or 'Why am I here; what is my purpose in life?' this book is a must!

Poonamallee thoughtfully warns about the commodification of mindfulness in its popular rise in today's leadership training and development industry, along with the limits of 'using' meditative practices to simply cope with personal stress or anxiety. Her alternative is a holistic approach to exploring and developing a sense of oneself, inwardly and outwardly, presently and in movement toward a future. She carefully integrates western science, eastern metaphysics, and narratives from her and her students' reflective experiences to give us a literal guide to discover and explore one's personal self, relational self, communal self and self in a life-journey.

Poonamallee rightfully notes that one can read this (and other) work to 'know about' mindfulness, but to 'understand' something real about it requires experiencing what results from actual meditative and self-reflective work. The inclusion of numerous guides and exercises that she has validated over decades of her research and practice is a valuable step toward supporting the reader to try out something so that they can discover and validate (or not) the beneficial results described so richly by the author and her trainees in this text."

Ronald Fry, PhD. *Professor, Case Western Reserve University*

"Expansive Leadership is a book with the serious objective of changing leadership perspectives with a fresh approach. It is imperative that readers read the opening pages carefully to understand context, learn the purpose and the benefits of reading the book. Inspiring that the author's note is, readers will move further into the chapters as their interest is tapped already. Techniques are well detailed, and a lay person can easily follow the routine. The journal towards the end of the book is very important and a good tool for the reader."

Viju Swaminathan, *Head of HR Consulting,*
Tate Leadership Development Consulting

"This book meticulously develops the concept of expansive leadership, and how to create that in one's life by embracing mental models needed for this approach. Dr. Poonamallee outlines a practical and easy-to-implement program that gives us all a chance to increase our expansive leadership for a greater good. Dr. P speaks extensively about the qualities of curiosity and kindness as paths to this transformational and holistic approach to leadership that no longer buys into the hierarchical top-down approach but embraces empowerment through a bottom-up approach to change.

This book to helps people to break away from previously embraced constricting identities, instead urges us all to embrace an existential journey that will lead to the expansive and inclusive leadership approach badly needed to address our present global dilemmas. Dr. Poonamallee does not shy away from the moral implications of mindfulness and leadership. This book does not offer the Mcmindfulness techniques which sometimes pops up in corporate settings these days, but takes us through a series of rather profound and penetrating insights to entice us along the journey that takes one from a egocentric, individualistic perspective to intra-personal transcendent relational self that is communal without being tribal, and takes both the individual, the organization and society a whole on a path of a renewal and integration."

Louise Kelly, PhD *author of "The Psychologist Manager:*
Success Models for Psychologies in Executive Positions,"
Professor Univ of La Vern

"At a time when COVID 19 has us under siege, each of us needs to adopt ways of centering ourselves in our core, to be fortified to foster and care for not just us but others. Latha maps out a bi-directional journey, simultaneously taking us deeper into ourselves and growing to include others and touching their lives meaningfully. Mindfulness and inclusiveness are woven together to create the new tapestry of Expansive leadership, a prosocial, altruistic and transformative model that the 21st century is in dire need of. As a model, expansive leadership opens up a personal, humanistic route to make oneself capable of transforming us to who we wish to be and how we wish to lead.

Using an intimate and inspiring style, Latha gently leads us through the personal growth process, helping us clarify the principles on which we base our identity and approach towards others. Through the many reflective yet grounding exercises, one is led to rethink our moral identities and recreate our mental models to rise up to our expansive – transcendental self. In the book, I found a secular and empowering approach to using mindfulness in leading self and others, anchored on reflection and progress."

Priya Rajeev, PhD. *Associate Professor,*
Indian Institute of Management, Kozhikode

"Dr. Poonamallee contributes a fresh, even path-breaking, take on how Mindfulness, Mental Models (e.g. the need for awareness of/critical reflection on how our individual-tribal-collective mental models profoundly shape behaviors that quickly follow), and Expansive Leadership (as compared to more conventional leadership approaches) can better equip us for life in today's highly diverse, closely networked, fast-changing, often conflict-riven social settings. The book is conversational and supported strongly by scholarship. It's an exciting approach that cleverly invites mindful reflection-and-learning."

Anita Howard, PhD. *Executive Coach and Organizational Consultant,*
Professor, Case Western Reserve University

"In this extraordinary book, Latha Poonamallee gives us the essence of 'mindfulness' and shows us how its powerful and broad implications create more effective leaders. She knows what she's talking about: Her years as a practitioner and first-person experiences demonstrate her credibility. Her research expertise builds a bullet-proof case for *Mindful Leadership* that rests on solid empirical evidence. Her years teaching the theory and practice of this new leadership model, in a variety of settings, give us insight into how accessible mindfulness is to us all. Considering the plethora of books on this topic over the past few years, it would have been easy for Poonamallee's leadership model to get lost in the noise. But she cuts through it effortlessly and, simultaneously, takes us by the grown-up hand to show us the steps for applying it in twenty-eight days."

Mark Lipton, PhD. *Professor of Management, The New School, and author of "Mean Men: The perversion of America's self-made man" and "Guiding Growth: How vision keeps companies on course"*

"Mindfulness is gaining ground as a means to deal with the troubled times we live in. As someone who has regained her equilibrium through mindfulness, I would urge you to adopt these simple practices in your everyday life. Dr. Poonamallee' lucid style made this book a ready reckoner for me to evolve into a self-assured practitioner. A must have on your bookshelf in your journey towards calm and inner peace."

Hastha Krishnan, CEO,
Tate Leadership Consulting & Trustee, The Ma Foi Foundation

Expansive Leadership

The structured 28-day mindfulness and contemplative journey presented in this book will help aspiring and current leaders to clarify their identities, and identify and reflect on their mental models to become more expansive leaders.

The present moment demands new ways of being, doing, and relating with the world. To meet this moment, we need fresh, collective, inclusive, and interdependent models of leadership and new approaches to leadership development. This book goes beyond the 'McMindfulness' often seen in mindful leadership books, to offer a multi-faceted approach to develop a more interconnected sense of self and interdependence-centric mindsets needed for expansive leadership, through mindfulness practice. Through this practice, leaders can cultivate the ability to make deliberate choices using slow thinking and overcome any unconscious and implicit biases that are the result of fast-thinking processes. Anchored in insights from over ten years of teaching mindfulness-based leadership development courses, this book is an invitation to explore how to be a leader in an expansive, inclusive, robust, and resilient way. The reader will have an opportunity to define and refine their identity, uncover their personal mental models, and conclude by developing their own leadership philosophy.

Leadership development professionals and teachers can adopt this for their students, coaching, and consulting clients.

Dr. Latha Poonamallee is Associate Professor, Chair of the Faculty of Management, and University Fellow at the New School in New York City. Latha's scholarship, teaching and practice centers generative organizing for radical change towards building a more just, equitable, sustainable, and prosperous world.

Expansive Leadership

Cultivating Mindfulness to Lead Self
and Others in a Changing World –
A 28-Day Program

Latha Poonamallee Ph.D.

Routledge
Taylor & Francis Group

NEW YORK AND LONDON

First published 2021
by Routledge
52 Vanderbilt Avenue, New York, NY 10017

and by Routledge
2 Park Square, Milton Park, Abingdon, Oxon OX14 4RN

Routledge is an imprint of the Taylor & Francis Group, an informa business

© 2021 Latha Poonamallee

Library of Congress Cataloging-in-Publication Data
Names: Poonamallee, Latha, author.
Title: Expansive leadership : cultivating mindfulness to lead self and others in a changing world - a 28-day program / Latha Poonamallee.
Description: New York, NY : Routledge, 2021. | Includes bibliographical references and index.
Identifiers: LCCN 2020052446 (print) | LCCN 2020052447 (ebook) | ISBN 9780367699758 (hbk) | ISBN 9780367699741 (pbk) | ISBN 9781003144083 (ebk)
Subjects: LCSH: Leadership. | Mindfulness (Psychology)
Classification: LCC BF637.L4 P63 2021 (print) | LCC BF637.L4 (ebook) | DDC 158/.4–dc23
LC record available at https://lccn.loc.gov/2020052446
LC ebook record available at https://lccn.loc.gov/2020052447

ISBN: 9780367699758 (hbk)
ISBN: 9780367699741 (pbk)
ISBN: 9781003144083 (ebk)

Typeset in Sabon
by Taylor & Francis Books

I dedicate this book to three men in my life without whom this book would not exist.

My late father, Sri. Chandrasekaran Poonamallee and my first mindfulness teacher. He prized knowledge, open-mindedness, and compassion. I was an emotional late bloomer and he was my buffer with the world. I miss him every day.

My husband and life partner, Al Curran, who with his everyday kindness and acts of service teaches me that love can be generous, free, and emancipatory.

My son, Viyan Poonamallee, is the center of my universe. We raise each other in love. Thank you for the gift of learning to love absolutely, unconditionally, and trustfully.

Contents

Illustrations

Figures

Tables

Bio of Dr. Latha Poonamallee

Dr. Latha Poonamallee is Associate Professor, Chair of Management Faculty, and Faculty Fellow at the New School in New York City. She also serves as the Editor in Chief of the Society for Advancement of Management's scholarly journal. Latha's scholarship and practice centers on generative organizing to build a more just, sustainable, and prosperous world. She is engaged in two primary topical areas.

How to decolonize, decapitalize, and demystify mindfulness and contemplative practice so it can be utilized to advance more expansive mental models and mindsets to lead social action and change in our complex world. She researches, teaches, and consults extensively on this topic.

Her second area of scholarship is on socio-tech innovation and entrepreneurship. She recently published the book, "Socio-Tech Innovation: Harnessing Technology for Social Good" with Palgrave Macmillan. She co-founded In-Med Prognostics, a neuroscience-AI social venture that brings affordable and accessible brain health tools to underserved markets. As Fulbright Fellow, she worked with the Botswana Civil Society, Botswana Government, US Embassy in Botswana, USAID, and the private sector in Botswana to develop a social entrepreneurship ecosystem and leadership capacity building for the civil society.

Dr. Poonamallee received her PhD in Organizational Behavior from Case Western Reserve University, USA.

LinkedIn: https://www.linkedin.com/in/nextfrontiersolutions

Figure 0.1 Dr. Latha Poonamallee

Foreword

Leaders existed long before the emergence of leadership theories. History is full of inspiring leaders who inspire us to transform our lives and communities. To emulate such leaders, we need to understand what makes them great leaders. One of the most endearing aspects of great leaders is their ability to connect to people from various walks of life. Their encounters with their followers full of stories of how personable they are. Simultaneously they invoke a sense of awe and connection that put everyone at ease. They are diligent and mindful of situated and complex stories of ourselves.

Mindful awareness is an essential ingredient of successful leaders. Mindful leadership is a growing area of research. Although the clinical and practitioner-oriented approach to mindful leadership is in vogue, Dr. Poonamallee's book provides a comprehensive, theory-driven, yet practitioner-friendly approach to mindful leadership. It emphasizes interconnectedness, interdependence, and a commitment to social change (Mahalingam, 2019). It addresses a significant gap in the growing body of research on mindful leadership. What are the challenges to becoming a mindful leader?

According to eminent Tibetan Buddhist master Dilgo Khyentse, diligence is vital for an awakened mind. Dilgo Khyentse (2007) defines diligence as the "joyous effort and active determination to carry out positive actions, without any expectations or self-satisfaction (p. 160)." Poonamallee argues that to be diligent, we must cultivate an expansive sense of self to overcome our self-centered and egocentric desires to pursue leadership for self-aggrandizement.

Becoming an expansive leader is a journey that starts with the stilling of the mind. According to Tibetan master teacher Kharak Gomchung (cited in Khyentse, 2007):

> In the mind of a beginner
> There is clarity, but no stability;
> To stop it being consigned to the wind of thoughts,
> Fasten it with the rope of mindfulness.

Anyone who tries to do a mindful meditation will empathize with Kharak Gomchung's warning. We all need to master the art of fastening our wandering mind with the rope of mindfulness.

Grounded on her research on the expansive self, Dr. Poonamallee has developed an excellent hands-on program on mindful leadership. To cultivate an expansive leadership, we have to cultivate mindfulness. Dr. Poonamallee's four-week program will guide us through the process of fastening our mind with the rope of mindfulness.

Dr. Poonamallee researches mindfulness and has years of experience teaching mindful leadership to various audiences. As an action researcher, there is a seamless connection between her research, practice, and teaching. The chasm between the knower and the process of knowing is a critical challenge for any teacher considering the heterogeneity in student learning styles. Dr. Poonamallee has handled this challenge admirably with a lot of compassion. Using her rich pedagogical experience, she has skillfully woven the personal narratives of transformations, which are insightful and a delight to read. These narratives are windows to myriad ways of learning and understanding mindfulness practices. These experiential learning narratives also provide a rich tapestry of embodying expansive leadership.

This book offers a unique, enriching account of what expansive leadership is and how to cultivate it. As a dedicated teacher, Dr. Poonamallee provides a rich array of practices that will benefit students with varying mastery of mindfulness. The book offers a robust roadmap to cultivating expansive mindful leadership. Expansive leadership embodies diligence with a commitment to making positive leadership changes for an inclusive, diverse, and equitable world.

Ram Mahalingam, PhD
Barger Leadership Institute Professor
Department of Psychology
Director, Barger Leadership Institute
Director, Mindful Dignity Lab
Senior Fellow, Michigan Society of Fellows
University of Michigan
Ann Arbor, MI 48109–1043

References

Khyentse, D. (2007). *The heart of compassion: The thirty-seven verses on the practice of a Bodhisattva*. Boston, MA: Shambala.

Mahalingam, R. (2019). Mindful Mindset, Interconnectedness, and Dignity. *Global Youth*, 1, 230–253.

Acknowledgements

This book wrote itself. I was merely the instrument fortunate enough to live and breathe this work. I owe a debt of gratitude to many for supporting me on this journey. All mistakes are mine.

- Hundreds of students and participants in my workshops and classes willing to experiment, risk, and stretch, without whom I couldn't have developed or tested the frameworks and tools I offer in this book.
- My graduate school professors Drs. Richard Boyatzis, David Cooperrider, and Ron Fry for their support.
- Drs. Anita Howard, Jaye Goosby, and Mark Lipton for reading my drafts and giving me insightful feedback. I cannot ask for better colleagues and friends.
- Nithya Niranjan and Yamuna Vittal, for reading early drafts and encouraging me that I can in fact write for regular audience.
- My colleague and friend, Prof. Anne Beffel for the inspiring work she does in contemplative art world.
- My friend and colleague, Cotter Christian, who is my partner in the Mindfulness @The New School project. Our weekly meetings were a balm to soothe my spirit during this difficult year.
- My LinkedIn connections who enthusiastically helped me in crafting the title of the book.
- My comrade and brother in mindfulness, Dr. Ram Mahalingam, who graciously wrote a foreword to the book.

Part 1

The Ground

Chapter 1

Preparing the Ground

Preparing

Close your eyes for a moment and let yourself take a deep breath. Deeper than you normally allow for. Imagine for a few moments that we are all interconnected parts of the same web of life; not just you and me as individuals and humans, but the universe at large. What kind of world would that be? What kind of organizations, communities, and societies would we create? What kind of relationships would we embed ourselves in and invest our time in? How would we make decisions? What kind of leadership would we need to foster and support that world? How do we nurture and develop that kind of leadership?

The present moment demands that we invent new ways of being, doing, and relating with the world; new ways to protect ourselves and the world from our own worst impulses to ensure that we don't exacerbate the fragility of the world we live in. To meet this moment, we need fresh, collective, inclusive, and interdependent models of leadership and new approaches to leadership development. Not just doing the same thing better but doing better things with our lives, resources, talents, and opportunities.

Grounded in my work on integrative mental models and identities,[1][2][3] I present the Expansive Leadership Model, as a 21st century alternative to the egocentric and tribal centric leadership models of yesteryears and provide a blueprint for how to use mindfulness and contemplative approaches for developing socially mindful, just, collective, and inclusive leadership. In recent years, mindfulness practice has been enthusiastically adopted by different organizations, sectors, and communities from educators[4] to therapists[5] and even business executives. The field of leadership development has seen its share of adoption of mindfulness as well.[6][7][8][9] Mindfulness and contemplative practice are effective tools for such an undertaking[10] because at the very minimum these approaches foster self-awareness and emotional self-regulation[11] that are foundational for effective leadership.

An unknown author wrote:

Between stimulus and response there is a space. In that space is our power to choose our response. In our response lies our growth and freedom.

Meditation and mindfulness practice nurture our ability to inhabit that space with power and agency. The ability to lead begins with the process of self-discovery, self-awareness, self-leadership, and discovering our connections to other people and the universe at large. Central to this framework is the practical mindfulness training which incorporates:

- Intentionality
- Authenticity
- Prosocial orientation
- Transformation
- Service.

Through mindfulness training, we learn how to cultivate attention and awareness that allows us to live all aspects of our lives with a great sense of skill, connection, openness, and balance. Paying attention to the activity of the mind for even a few minutes yields powerful and potentially valuable information. Our capacity to listen deeply, to make informed decisions, to effectively handle stress, to ignite innovation, and to access previously untapped resources and apply them rely on our capacity to be mindful and present. When we are fully present in the moment, we optimize our capacity for self-awareness, self-regulation, and relationship management. The primary tenet is *Respond not React.*

Mindfulness is more commonly used for leadership development in instrumental ways such as stress and anxiety reduction, improving resilience, increasing attention and concentration – mostly all towards being more productive in workplace contexts. This approach bypasses the original intent that underlies mindfulness practice and shortchanges the practitioner. The original intent of all mindfulness and contemplative practice is to develop insight, compassion, critical inquiry towards an ethical life (*dharma*) – especially in the Buddhist tradition that permeates the mindfulness utilization in contemporary western world.[12] By focusing primarily if not solely on the immediate priorities of individual pain reduction, and people's effectiveness in the capitalistic and material worlds, and by overlooking the moral and spiritual questions, most contemporary approaches to mindfulness-based leadership development bypass the spiritual intent[13] and truncate an individual's capacity for holistic development.[14] Welwood refers to Chogyam Trungpa Riponche's term "spiritual materialism" or "*the tendency to commodify spirituality itself in service of our own ego-clinging*":

No matter what the practice or teaching, ego loves to wait in ambush to appropriate spirituality for its own survival and gain.[15]

Further, the contemporary focus also obfuscates the persistent structural inequities where the individual experience is not explored in the context of social identities. Without context and an examination of how people challenge, engage, or are silently complicit in the perpetuation of existing inequalities and the destruction of the natural environment.[16]

Removed from its moral and communal contexts and lacking in ethical frameworks[17] and expectations,[18] contemporary mindfulness practices – especially in corporate or corporate like settings – is the nexus of cultural appropriation, commodification, and white supremacy. Like Gandhi's *Satyagraha* – which in its core is an active fight for truth[19] – is often mischaracterized as passive political resistance, the so-called mindfulness revolution[20] has moved the practice from its original purpose of liberation and enlightenment to quelling resistance and serving profits. This phenomenon of McMindfulness[21] or McDonaldization of mindfulness movement is exemplified by the Time Magazine featuring blond, white women on covers of two issues exalting the mindfulness revolution.[22] The fact that the two issues were separated by a decade demonstrates how entrenched this approach has become. The most well-known mindful leadership teachers are all uniformly white, corporate, and promote mindfulness as a way for people to cope with their busy, stressful world and contribute to the bottom-line rather than fortifying and supporting practitioners in challenging fundamental assumptions about the world in which we live. No doubt, a leader needs a calm space to recharge, but to focus solely on that as an outcome of this "mindfulness revolution" is narcissistic, self-referential, and irresponsible. This book proposes a multi-faceted mindfulness approach that takes a whole-person approach including the emotional, cognitive, embodied, experiential, moral and spiritual realms with an explicit goal of facilitating a more interconnected sense of self and expansive mindsets. In addition, this process leverages critical reflection around social identities and mental models that define how we engage with others and the world to look at ourselves anew. It takes bravery and resilience to face up to and sit with negative emotions such as shame and guilt that are bound to occur during such a critical examination. Mindfulness practice can help make sense of and process those negative emotions with resilience.

Growing up in a traditional South Indian brahmin family, stories of sages who had the power to will themselves into *samadhi* (meditative trance consciousness) through *dhyana* (meditation) and even connect to the future and past of the universe in that state were stock bedtime stories of my childhood. Throughout my teens and early twenties, I struggled to reconcile what was even then a deep fascination with contemplative practice and my progressive, feminist, anti-caste, anti-bigotry stance. To me, it all seemed part of the same package and I wanted nothing to do with it. I was in my mid-twenties when I started to meditate in earnestness and then continued to deepen my practice over the next two decades when I also obtained a doctorate in organizational behavior and was teaching leader-ship development in universities and consulting with a few organizations. Pieces started to click together; my personal meditation practice and professional calling of supporting people development merged. Later, when I started to teach by myself as a newly minted faculty member, I first taught the class as I was taught to teach. I have been experimenting and playing with the curriculum over the years to make it my own and address some of my concerns around the 'development' part. For example, I taught an entire semester once using popular Hollywood movies. This experimentation continued until my own 'aha' moment – using mindfulness and contemplative approaches as a pedagogy for leadership development.

Even though I owed much of my personal growth in emotional self-awareness and self-regulation to my mindfulness practice that started over 20 years ago, it didn't dawn on me that I could and should utilize it to teach leadership development until around ten years ago. The response to my experimentation with just one module of three weeks was so encouraging that I retooled the entire curriculum around mindfulness. Having taught it many times to different audiences, now I feel confident that I have distilled the essence, refined the process, and clarified and connected the underlying pedagogical principles that I wanted to share it with others who would like to apply it in their own self-development or in their leadership development practice.

I wished to create a mindfulness-based leadership development program particularly focused on cultivating mental models that are morally expansive and interdependence-centric and less egocentric and narrowminded or plagued by -isms. My goal was to develop a transformative, whole-person approach that considers leadership as a layered, complex phenomenon blending individual and structural transformation processes. This was partly in response to the competency approach to leadership development that focuses on behaviors and not at the underlying mental models and mindsets. I designed and implemented with the knowledge that mental models can be changed, and we can all cultivate more interdependent identities and prosocial mental models while acknowledging that we co-hold occasionally conflicting mental models and deal with complex and nuanced choices. Mindfulness practice is an appropriate choice to further this end because it also increases the capacity for cognitive complexity.[23] The program was developed over a ten-year period with different audience groups ranging from undergraduate students in engineering, technology, and business to graduate students in design, architecture, management, leadership and practitioners including managers, consultants, and social and environmental activists. I provide a glimpse into their experience through quotes drawn from their journals to bring to life the concepts and practices.

Like the Bodhisattva who delay their own salvation out of compassion for others, a good leader transcends their personal egocentricism.

Sometimes we forget that iconic (and altruistic) leaders such as Mahatma Gandhi, Dr. Martin Luther King, and President Nelson Mandela were also flesh and blood humans like the rest of us. Meditation practice grounds us in the shared human condition – capacity for greatness, altruism, and pro-social mindfulness simultaneously co-existing with egocentricism, fear, anxiety, and the impulse to dehumanize the 'other.' The practice allows us to own our greatness while being brave enough to face our ignorant and ignoble impulses. It allows us to make a deliberate choice through slow thinking that helps us overcome our unconscious and implicit biases. The moment of pause is essential to slow our thinking so we can transcend the rote script by which we are all trained in our formative years and rewarded in adult years.

I invite you to join this journey and explore how to be a leader in an expan-sive, inclusive, robust, and resilient way using mindfulness practice in an iterative and cyclical way from individual to structural and back in an integrative manner. You will have an opportunity to define and refine your iden-tity, uncover your personal mental models, and conclude with developing your own leadership philosophy. The book has been designed to introduce you to a new model of leadership while facilitating experiential explora-tions of the concepts through mindfulness practice. I have provided key references as endnotes to further your exploration into the academic research on which this model stands.

The book is divided into four parts. Parts 1, 2 and 3 provide the basics of this model filled with experiential exercises including application in the real world and how to infuse mindfulness in your everyday life. Part 4 is a structured journey through the model. I recommend following the 28-day plan that has been designed to give you an opportunity to systematically follow the guidelines and prompts and traverse through the personal to the communal to the structural using a combination of meditation practices, activities, and journal prompts. However, you should feel free to dip in or dig deep as you desire.

Foundation to this work is practice. No amount of reading will make up for experience. It is like reading love stories to find love. Yes, reading love stories, poetry, and watching rom-com movies may make you more open to being loved, but it doesn't mean you will find love or fall in love ... if you don't also put yourself out there, willing to risk heartbreak, and try. It helps to approach mindfulness practice with an understanding that this is one of the hardest things most of us may have undertaken. Despite my decades of practice, every time it is brand new. But that is why mindfulness can help us cultivate a beginner's mindset. However, there is no need to exoticize or mystify it. Being mindful and cultivating mindfulness is accessible to all of us. That is the paradox. There is no there there.

If you want to use this framework to facilitate leadership development for others, you need to have experienced at least some of the things the participants in your program will undergo. To understand the initial challenges and resistance, you need to practice, practice, practice too. Feel how long five minutes can feel like when one needs to sit. I strongly encourage that you complete the program yourself first before offering it to others, but the book is laid out in detail for easy adoption and implementation. If you take the latter option, make a commitment to your personal practice while you are facilitating others' growth using the methodology. Share your experiences in the conversations you facilitate to normalize resistance.

Notes

1 Poonamallee, L. C., & Goltz, S. M. (2014). Beyond Social Exchange Theory: an Integrative Look at Transcendent Mental Models for Engagement. *Integral Theory*, 10(1), 63–90.

2 Poonamallee, L., Harrington, A., Nagpal, M., & Musial, A. (2018). Improving Emotional Intelligence through Personality Development: The Effect of the Smartphone App based Dharma Life Program on Emotional Intelligence. *Frontiers in Psychology*.

3 Poonamallee, L. C. (2011). Impact of Collective Socio-Ecological Beliefs and Values on Societal Compassion in Disaster Management. Academy of Management Best Paper Proceedings, San Antonio, TX.

4 Beer, L. E., Rodriguez, K., Taylor, C., Martinez-Jones, N., Griffin, J., Smith, T. R., Lamar, M., & Anaya, R. (2015). Awareness, integration and interconnectedness contemplative practices of higher education professionals. *Journal of Transformative Education*, 13, 161–185. doi:10.1177/1541344615572850.

5 Wimmer, L., Bellingrath, S., & Stockhausen, L. v. (2016). Cognitive Effects of Mindfulness Training. *Frontiers in Psychology*. doi:10.3389/fpsyg.2016.01037.

6 Baron, L. (2016), Authentic leadership and mindfulness development through action learning, *Journal of Managerial Psychology*, 31(1), 296–311. doi:10.1108/JMP-04-2014-0135.

7 Beekum, S. (2016). Mindfulness and Leadership: A Critical Reflection. *Business and Management Studies*, 2. doi:10.11114/bms.v2i1.1190.

8 Tuleja, E. A.(2014). Developing Cultural Intelligence for Global Leadership Through Mindfulness. *Journal of Teaching in International Business*, 25(1), 5–24, doi:10.1080/08975930.2014.881275.

9 Eisenbeiss, S., & Knippenberg, D. (2014). On ethical leadership impact: The role of follower mindfulness and moral emotions. *Journal of Organizational Behavior*, 36. doi:10.1002/job.1968.

10 Allen, T. D., & Kiburz, K. M. (2012). Trait mindfulness and work-family balance among working parents: The mediating effects of vitality and sleep quality. *Journal of Vocational Behavior*, 80, 372–379. doi:10.1016/j.jvb.2011.09.002.

11 Vago, D. R., & Silbersweig, D. A. (2012). Self-awareness, self-regulation, and self-transcendence (S-ART): a framework for understanding the neurobiological mechanisms of mindfulness. *Frontiers in Human Neuroscience*, 6, 296. doi:10.3389/fnhum.2012.00296.

12 Hickey, W. S. (2010). Meditation as medicine: A critique. *CrossCurrents*, 60(2), 168–184. doi:10.1111/(ISSN)1939–3881.

13 Masters, R. A. (2010). *Spiritual bypassing: When spirituality disconnects us from what really matters*. Berkeley, CA: North Atlantic Books.

14 Fossella, T. (2011). Human nature, Buddha nature: On spiritual bypassing, relationship, and the dharma: An interview with John Welwood. *Tricycle Magazine*, Spring.

15 Welwood, J. (2002). *Toward a psychology of awakening*. Boston, MA: Shambhala.

16 Sherell, J., & Simmer-Brown, J. (2017). Spiritual bypassing in the contemporary mindfulness movement. *ICEA Journal*, 1(1), 75–93. https://www.academia.edu/34353436/Spiritual_Bypassing_in_the_Contemporary_Mindfulness_Movement#:~:text=Whenever%20the%20practice%20is%20engaged,spiritual%20bypassing%20attitudes%20and%20motivations.

17 Loy, D. (2003). *The great awakening: A Buddhist social theory*. Boston, MA: Wisdom.

18 Queen, C. S. (2002). Engaged Buddhism: Agnosticism, interdependence, globalization. In C. S. Prebish, & M. Baumann (Eds.), *Westward dharma: Buddhism beyond Asia*. Berkeley, CA: University of California Press.

19 Poonamallee, L. C. (2010). Advaita (non-dualism) as metatheory: a constellation of ontology, epistemology and praxis, Steven Wallis (Ed.). *Integral Review*, 6(3), 190–200.

20 Pickett, K. (2014). The mindful revolution. *Time*, January 24.

21 Purser, R., & Loy, D. (2013). Beyond McMindfulness. *Huffington Post*. Retrieved from http://www.huffingtonpost.com/ron-purser/beyond-mcmindfulness_b_3519289.html.

22 Sherell, J., & Simmer-Brown, J. (2017). Spiritual bypassing in the contemporary mindfulness movement. *ICEA Journal*, 1(1), 75–93. https://www.academia.edu/34353436/Spiritual_Bypassing_in_the_Contemporary_Mindfulness_Movement#:~:text=Whenever%20the%20practice%20is%20engaged,spiritual%20bypassing%20attitudes%20and%20motivations.

23 Youngvorst, L. J., & Jones, S. M. (2017). The Influence of Cognitive Complexity, Empathy, and Mindfulness on Person-Centered Message Evaluations. *Communication Quarterly*, 65(5), 549–564. doi:10.1080/01463373.2017.1301508.

Chapter 2

Letting Go Not Leaning In: Begin with the Breath

For the uninitiated, meditation can be a daunting proposition. People come to the practice with several misconceptions. They think it is an emptying of the mind and worry that they won't be able to stop thinking or feeling or whatever it is that they think they should be able to control. We think we should strive to resist our thoughts. But the cruel joke is that what we resist tends to persist.

One participant in my program writes about their concerns:

> I was always drawn away from anything that involved meditation. My mind is constantly spinning with different thoughts, concerns, anxieties, and ideas in my head that I never believed it would be feasible for me.

An ancient Tibetan parable refers to this predicament as the monkey that wouldn't go away. When one is tasked not to think of a monkey to achieve nirvana, all one can think of is monkeys – monkeys in the house, monkeys in the forests, monkeys stealing stuff, monkeys jumping into water, monkeys playing with each other, and so on and so forth. All your thoughts are about trying to banish the monkeys from your thoughts! Here is a peek into my wandering mind at moments like these. I'm trying not to think of monkeys but instead, that's all I do. My inner dialogue goes like this:

> What would you do if that monkey comes into your home? If you shoo it, will it go away? Can you toss a banana out to the porch and lure him away? If you close all the doors to keep the monkeys away, then your air is stale, and your house is too warm for comfort. If Hanuman is Monkey God, aren't you chasing god away by shooing a monkey away? Will the monkey bring more of his friends to eat all your bananas that are ripening in your garden? Can I hose the monkey away? Does a monkey respond to water? Seriously, is a monkey scared of water? Do monkeys carry fleas? Do they bite? Are they dangerous? Maybe I should google to find out more about monkeys. Are they

deliberately diabolical? Or just naturally mischievous? Can they give me rabies? What happens if I get bitten by a monkey? What happens if I get bitten by a monkey on a weekend and my local clinic is not open and I need to go to the hospital?

So many monkey thoughts intrude when you are told that your objective is to banish all thoughts regarding monkeys. People with a high achievement orientation[1] particularly tend struggle with how to sit back in calmness and let something come to them. Those of us like this need and relish the sense of control that comes from being able to make things happen. I speak from personal experience. What makes us effective in the profane world becomes a burden in the contemplative world. That type of striving gets in the way of letting go even momentarily. Leaning in comes in the way of letting go. In my twenties, I was tangentially involved with a sea turtle rescue group on the coast of the Bay of Bengal that gave night tours to local families to teach them about the animal. On some nights, families were fortunate enough to see eggs either being laid or hatching. On others, nothing. Occasionally, families would get upset. They didn't understand that this was not a zoo; we couldn't guarantee a sighting! Sometimes, meditating is just as frustrating. We put in the effort and ... nothing.

I always begin with the breath because I find breath to be most accessible. We are all already breathing anyways. It is not about stopping or banishing something. It is about making your breath your friend and paying attention to it. With this practice, you are just invited to notice your breath. No need for anything else. No lateral expansion of the lungs. No deep breathing. No pranayama. No lion's breath. Just begin by observing your breath. If you forget to observe and lose track, you come back to it when you notice that you are not observing anymore. It is as simple as that. But even then, it is not that simple.

G, one of the practitioners in my program, writes about her initial frustrations:

> I will be honest; I did not practice mindfulness meditation every day this week until today as I was completing this week's assignment. I did the two breathing exercises, one in the morning after going to the bathroom and then in the evening right before I started my reading assignments. I hated every possible moment. I restarted at least four times both sessions because I opened my eyes less than halfway through each session, I sometimes missed the cue to breathe, I couldn't sit still in my chair, my fingers and legs were fidgety, my back ached, and my mind wandered. I was not happy with this first attempt.

Even though it seems like she was struggling with the practice, paradoxically, it was through the struggle she engaged in the practice. She observed. She noticed little details. She was mindful of her fidgetiness in the moment and noticed how her back ached and her mind wandered. It was not the non-judgmental awareness we hope to cultivate through meditation and mindfulness practice, but still she paid attention and became aware of her internal state and how that manifested in her body. To me that is the crux of mindfulness practice. It is about progress not perfection.

G writes about her continued progress:

> When I was able to finally slow down and do the breathing exercises, I felt more relaxed. I noticed that my mind wandered from time to time, but I was able to bring it back to the breath. When I meditate, I am often hyper-aware of my inner struggles with patience, accepting uncertainty and the unknown, as well as letting go of my desire to control every aspect of my future. I notice my subtle resistance to the practice at first, as well as the moment when I am able to give in and let go of my over-active brain. I try to be present and stop planning, just be in my body and stick with the rhythm of my breath. Despite feeling stressed about stopping the flow of my day for it or taking time away from other productive tasks, I do enjoy the practice and look forward to continuing it.

Everyone's experience is personal, different, and unique even though the practice itself is universal. An artist who participated in the program wrote about her first-time meditation thus:

> First time I practiced it was early in the morning before my first cup of tea. It was 6:00 am and I had woken up to the light of the sun's rays slipping through the blinds of my window. It was just a couple of days after having registered for the class. I was super excited about practicing meditation and so I did that holy morning. I sat up straight on my bed, crossed my legs and shut my eyes. I was positioned such that I was directly facing the sun. The sharp rays of the sun made me feel awake as never before. Since this was my first-time meditating, voluntarily, I went at it with ease and decided to keep my eyes shut and zone out all my problems and just concentrate on my breath for as long as possible. At first when I started, I found it extremely difficult to stop thinking as I felt like I had a rush of the most random thoughts going through at the very moment. Only a few minutes later, was I able to get a hold of them and ended up with a feeling of complete silence on my mind. I stayed that way for a few minutes and tried to concentrate on how I breathe. After a good 15–17 minutes (approx.), I found myself to be even more energetic than before. I felt happier. I did not know what it was, but I just had a different level of energy and motivation that

morning. Reflecting on that entire day, my day did go well and very rarely did I find myself cribbing about small things.

Part of my goal in writing this book is to demystify how to apply mindfulness in real life contexts. Sometimes we are terrified of breathing mindfully. What we do on automaticity becomes a struggle the moment we begin to pay attention.

A participant writes:

> Monday meditation was terrible. I was not able to connect with myself because I had a lot of ideas and thoughts that came to my mind. Besides that, I had more distractions on the outside because my nephews were still on vacation. However, I tried to not lose my sense of purpose of continuing with the practice, so I continued with the same energy and attitude. Finally, I couldn't find my personal space where I can start my meditation every day, so I decided to do it at night in the room that I was sharing with my niece.

It is not an uncommon experience. Our goal is to move from fearful to trustful breathing. I find that characterizing breath as the best friend that never leaves our side makes it easier to trust our breath and ourselves. I jokingly say that breathing is better than the alternative – not breathing. Breath mediation is an invitation to struggle less and embrace more of what is already happening.

Here is a good story about a manager/new father describing his emerging practice:

> This has been my first time practicing mindfulness consistently night after night. I have tried it in the past as I heard great things about it and how healthy it can be for you, but never consistently. Over the past few nights (since the beginning of this class), after the practice of mindfulness, I find myself more relaxed and in a better mood. It has gotten to the point that I look forward to this practice. I find myself doing it in the late evening, after a long day of work and responsibilities. My son is asleep, and I find myself with no distractions. In my opinion, this is the perfect time to do this practice as it is a time when I have a lot on my mind. I am thinking about everything that happened during the day and thinking about what I need to do tomorrow. Having these twenty minutes to focus on the present at this specific moment in the day is extremely helpful. I have found that I struggle to keep my mind from wandering. When I recognize this, I remind myself to focus on my breathing and to how my body is feeling and try my best to remain in the present time.

By reclaiming our breath, we reclaim our sacred connection to ourselves and the world.

I invite you to join a brief breath meditation. A longer breath meditation is provided in Part 4.

Breathing Meditation 1

Sit comfortably

Keep your spine in its natural form. You don't have to be stressed. You are in a calm place. You can sit on the floor or chair – whatever is comfortable.

Close your eyes
We are just going to try breathing meditation
Inhale ...
Exhale ...
Inhale ...
Exhale ...
If your mind wanders, gently bring it back to your breath
Inhale ...
Exhale ...
You are already breathing
We all do
You are doing something natural
Nothing forced
Just breathe in and breathe out
Breathe in ...
Breathe out ...
See if you can focus on your breath
Just breathe in and breathe out
Breathe in ...
Breathe out ...
Your mind might wander
It is okay. No need to beat yourself up about it
It is okay if your mind wanders
Just gently bring it back to your breath
Breath is your best friend
It never leaves your side
Breathe in ...
Breathe out ...
Breathe in ...
Breathe out ...
When you are ready, gently open your eyes

******

To do: Brief Breath Meditation

If you are a novice, try the brief breath meditation above.

If you are an experienced practitioner, try the longer breath meditation practice or do your own breathing meditation or find one on an app or any website.

How did it feel? Was it easy? Was it difficult? Was it your first time? Or not?

Note

1 https://psychology.fas.harvard.edu/people/david-mcclelland.

Chapter 3

Introducing Expansive Leadership

There is no doubt that we are at a key inflection point of this century. We are gripped in a global pandemic that is predicted to leave an economic devastation that could rival the Great Depression and we are faced with the deep fissures in our socio-economic realities and the unrelenting burden our society's underprivileged carry for the rest of us. Paradoxically, it has also engendered the collective moral outrage of people of all hues and colors against the police brutality in the case of George Floyd and other black lives that must matter but were lost. It has brought together people of all ages around the world to challenge the entrenched and structural racism and around their desire for a voice and for justice for all. The pandemic and the civil unrest also highlight how much we humans crave connection, related-ness, mutuality, fellowship, and conviviality. Colleagues who are self-declared introverts surprise me by calling and wanting to Facetime and videoconference. Those who thought that work was merely a way to pay bills are surprised by how much of their social needs were met by their colleagues at work. The moment has showcased elected leaders such as New York Gov. Andrew Cuomo who – despite his flailing in the early stages of the pandemic and his pre Covid-19 reputation of being a bully – has shown up for his people with daily briefings exemplifying leadership in action, and Michigan Gov. Gretchen Whitmer whose brave policies saved tens of thousands of lives in her home state. Jacinda Arden, Prime Minister of New Zealand, lauded for leading one of the most effective response efforts by any country head, demonstrated that empathy is a key leadership principle during crisis. It has also brought to the fore young activists who have organized protests for the Black Lives Matter and Climate Justice movements. But the moment has also exposed the lack of leadership by President Donald Trump who seems to be simply incapable of mustering any empathy or concern for those who suffer and those who protest or lead in a way to promote unity and mutual understanding.

History provides mixed evidence about our capacity to learn and grow from these events that shake us to the core. The Great Depression was followed by the New Deal and World War II was followed by the Long

Peace. The New Deal was made possible by exemplary and decisive leadership by FDR. The Long Peace was facilitated by structural interventions aimed at poverty reduction and women's empowerment among other things. History also shows us that charismatic leaders can sometimes ascend to the top by appealing to people's baser instincts and raw emotions, leaders who were duly elected leaders but subsequently interested only in their own power and wealth, and immoral leaders who are divisive and corrosive to the societal well-being, and cause untold damage to their communities and organizations. My New School colleague, Mark Lipton, has written a scathing account of the ascendance of such narcissistic mean men in corporate America. The present moment is also an object lesson on how values and assumptions, leadership, communication, and changes in social systems are inextricably tied together. The time is ripe to reflect on the kind of world we wish to inhabit, the kind of world we must leave for our children and grandchildren, the kind of leaders we hope to be led by, the kind of leaders we want to be, and the kind of leaders we wish to develop.

To do: Analyze a Leader
Think of a leader you know – real, fictional, dead or alive.

- Select a specific decision that they made or an action they undertook and identify what drove the decision or action.
- How did the decision or action affect those around them?
- How do you think they related to those who were affected by their action?
- Do you think they served or serve a larger purpose?
- Would you call them a moral person?
- Are they a good leader?

Expansive Leadership, Mental Models, and Identities

Despite the recent disturbing developments in the form of the rise of political fundamentalism in several countries, the Covid-19 pandemic, and the ensuing economic insecurity, and what seems like a rejuvenated commitment to white, male, and class supremacy in certain quarters, at no point in history have we been more global and less tribal as a human race. We always talk about history as if it belongs to the past. We are currently living through it – a historic moment. The world needs leaders who know how to transcend tribal affiliations, model those actions, and possess the mindsets for building broad-based support for collective action across -isms and divides. The Expansive Leadership model is a robust response to this need. Expansive leaders recognize the interconnected nature of our worlds and lives and adopt a broader, more morally expansive view of life, its meaning, and our relationship with the world. They are collaborative, critically reflective, intergenerational, equitable, emotionally intelligent, intentional, and inclusive.

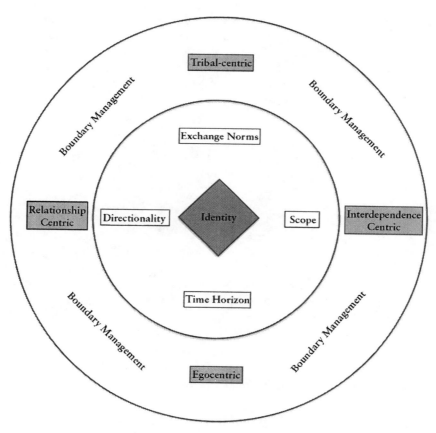

Figure 3.1 Expansive Mental Models

Expansive Leadership, Identity, and Mental Models

- Identity shapes our mental models.
- Mental models are made up of three aspects:

  a exchange norms (how we engage with others)
  b directionality of relationships
  c our perceived scope of impact and responsibility.

- There are four different levels of identity and associated mental models:

  a Individual/Egocentric
  b Interpersonal/Relationship-centric
  c Communal/Tribal-centric
  d Expansive/Interdependence-centric

- Because we are not just one thing, we sometimes deal with the messiness of having different mental models at the same time.
- When we deal with individuals or collectives with different mental models, we need to decide whether we do boundary-spanning or boundary-setting activities. This is also mediated by our access to power.
- Expansive leaders tend to ground their leadership actions in benevolence and interdependent-centric identity.

Constructing and Deconstructing Identities

Identity is how we define ourselves, in relation to other people, other living beings, the physical environment, and the universe at large.[1] How we define ourselves influences how we lead. But our identity is not a monolith;[2] it is composed of different levels and dimensions.[3] Part of our identity is personal, which is about us an individual (who am I?), part of it is made up of bits that are social (who are our people?) and partly structural (how does our belonging facilitate or constrain our power and agency?). In the ensuing chapters, you will have an opportunity to learn more about how you define your own identity and how that shapes your own actions as a leader.

In sum, our identity shapes our mental models that in turn influence our leadership actions and behaviors. Our identity determines four key aspects about how we engage with the world: *Relationship Directionality, Scope of Impact, Time Horizon* and *Exchange Norms.*

Egocentric or Individual identity → Self/Ego → Short Term Orientation → Transactional → Me Vs the World

When we operate from our egocentric or individual identity, we tend to be focused only on ourselves, mostly on short-term outcomes; our directionality of relationships is Me Vs the World and therefore we engage in mostly transactional norms of exchange.

> Interpersonal or Relational Identity → Self/Immediate others → Short-/Medium-Term orientation → Benevolent for a small group of people, transactional for others → Us Vs the World

When we operate from our interpersonal or relational identity, we tend to care about ourselves and our close or immediate others, including our family and team members, etc., with whom we have close or frequent contact. We look beyond the short-term to medium-term time horizons and extend benevolence in our norms of exchange to select close people and remain transactional with others who are outside of relationship bubble. When we operate in this mode, we adopt an Us Vs Them (instead of Me Vs the World) stance in our engagement.

> Tribal-centric or communal identity → Self/Select others, tribes → Short-/Medium-Term Orientation → Benevolent for select others, transactional for others →Us Vs the World

When we operate from tribal or communal identity, we see ourselves as part of a bigger whole than our immediate family or team and develop strong affective bonds with people who share our history, geography, interests, or some such tribal identity. In this mental model, we extend benevolence to larger group of people who belong to our in-group that is a bit or even substantially wider than our immediate family or team but stay transactional with the out-group members and operating in the Us Vs Them mentality. This leads to more boundary setting with outsiders and benevolence with our in-group members.

> Interdependence-centric or Expansive identity → Self/Immediate others/Unrelated others/Distant Strangers/Universe at Large → Long-Term Orientation → Benevolent → Complex, Interconnected, Me in the world

When we operate from universal identity or interdependence centric identity, we see ourselves as part of the larger universe. We are benevolent to the world at large including distant strangers. We take a much longer-term orientation and adopt a more expansive, complex, and interconnected view of ourselves in the world. It is important to remember that these mental models co-exist in most of us leading to our inner struggle of how to reconcile our personal interests with our moral responsibility for the others.

Identification with the Universe

Centuries' worth of empirical evidence show that people can and do transcend individual and interpersonal orientation for more collectivist concerns driven by expansive mental models. Do you ever wonder why non-Jews put themselves at risk to rescue Jews during World War II? Or how did Nelson Mandela treat the prison guards who held him captive for decades with compassion? Monroe (1996) found that the most shared quality among all those who rescued Jews during World War II was a "feeling of one shared human family."[4] Their identification as human transcended other narrower ethnic, national, and religious identities. People routinely give up individualistic notions for their family, friends, organizations they work in and churches they worship at, and demonstrate their capacity for altruism through volunteering for causes that move them.[5] They donate in response to others' suffering even when they don't know the sufferers themselves.[6] They transcend individual and interpersonal preoccupations and preferences for meeting the needs of their tribes and communities. McFarland and collaborators have done substantial work on an adjacent concept that they call "Identification With All Humanity."[7] This broad and expansive identification is unrelated to religiosity making it accessible to people of every faith and no faith. Regular mindfulness practice is a proven way to access this type of expansive identification.

Expansive leaders are grounded more in this type of interdependence-centered identity with moral expansiveness[89] and engage in prosocial behaviors. They are concerned about the planet, global humanitarian values, and support universal human rights. People with such expansive identities tend to value the lives of those who are in the out-groups as much as those in the in-groups[10] and less ethnocentric.[11] They are less prone to social domination orientation[12] and more prone to prosocial and altruistic orientation. Their dominant mental models are not based on self-interest driven but draw on abstract principles such as equality, justice, diversity, and views individuals, organizations, and systems as ecologically and socially embedded actors. Because expansive leaders operate from more interdependence-centric models, they consider the impact of their decisions on a larger set of stakeholders. It requires the capacity for cognitive complexity and perspective taking.[13] For example, a business owner who makes decisions based a broader array of deliberative variables such as financial implications, social benefits, and environmental impacts, and a variety of stakeholder groups, in place of a traditional and unidimensional understanding of business, needs to co-hold and balance conflicting priorities. We know we need leaders who are emotionally and socially intelligent. But we also need our leaders not to be egocentric or tribal-centric and to work for the good of the entire community. Our time calls for leaders who understand that their choices have long-term implications and that they are responsible for something beyond the immediate gratification. Me in the world. Me and the world.

The Modern Tribes

Most effective leaders are not transactional.[14] They are at the very least tribal, as in cultivating collective identities for a select set of people – for example, organizational identity.[15] Transactional leaders are mostly concerned about what they get out of something, how they look, and how to protect their personal power. Their orientation is Me Vs the World. Tribal centric leaders tend to have a bit more of an expansive notion of their scope of impact compared to the egocentric leaders. They think more in terms of Us Vs Them; demonstrating collective orientation for organizational members or members of affiliation – could be a sports team, fans of Star Wars, or players of the video game, Hollow Knight. Or they all work for the same employer; graduated from the same alma mater or share a profession. In today's diverse world, tribe members may not all look the same, but the notion of a tribe is not vastly different. They think of themselves not just as individuals but as members of a tribe or collective and they look at the impact of their actions and decisions on the group.

For many of us today, our tribes are not just those related by blood or kinship. Tribes can be made up of members with similar ideologies, experiences, or even similar taste in music, movies, or arts.[16] When we operate from this orientation, we tend to be more open to suspending our transactional norms for those in our in-groups because our ties with those folks are not just rational but also emotional and psychic. All types of organizations, including private corporations, political parties, religious organizations, fan clubs, non-profits and the military, depend on this type of affective commitment from their stakeholders. Research consistently shows that money (transactional norms) is insufficient to engender organizational commitment and citizenship behaviors by individuals. Therefore, organizations invest in encouraging shared identity and shared culture to promote organizational citizenship behaviors by which employees suspend the transactional norms of job for money with their employees and co-workers, hence moving from the first circle of egocentricism to the third circle of tribalism. Other examples include universities that try to build these emotional bonds for students and alumni, and some professional associations and industries that create a similar sense of kinship and ties that bind the people to the profession and ensure ongoing professionalization of newcomers. Such organizational or tribal sets of in-group identification result in more of an Us Vs Them mentality towards members of the out-groups.

Evolutionary theory explains this view that actors operating in this model do so because they have better chances at survival.[17] Such behavior allows sharing of resources[18] and supporting those who share blood relations[19] or similar identity systems or mental models lead to the preservation of the tribe or extended family or the institution. The focus here is short- to medium-term orientation and hierarchical relations based on power, ownership and negotiating belongingness. Although productive and meaningful in the short and medium term, its narrow awareness of scope of impact and limited relational directionality gets manifested in an Us Vs Them mentality and is likely to create problems in the long term, especially in complex situations and problems that need to take into account criteria other than tribal bonds. At an organizational level, this model may include organizational behaviors such as stakeholder relationships, responsiveness to customers, and employee well-being and health. Organizations operating on this mental model may define their identity as more than economic machines and may include internal and external stakeholders such as employees and customers thus going beyond their fiduciary responsibility. However, these are instrumental cultures trying to maximize the benefit to one group or firm even if at the cost of another system such as competitors, community, etc. While more humane at the tribal level, beyond one's tribe, it is still exploitative, competitive, and creates a win-lose paradigm.

Expansive leaders develop and apply a more complex view of the world – them in the world – so they look at their scope of impact more broadly because they understand that their decisions and actions have far reaching consequences and also care about the impact of their decisions on others who may not be as visible or may not belong to the select tribal affiliations. Like most of us, expansive leaders may be wary of strangers who are not like themselves, people with whom they do not share similar histories or kinship, but they do the emotional work needed for connection and are willing to risk extending benevolence. Grounded in the connection they feel to the universe and all of life, they exercise the moral imagination required to develop empathy and compassion for those with whom we don't seem to share that much in common. They deliberately and intentionally, if not automatically, suspend transactional norms in how they lead with 'the other.' This is crucial for restoring equity and going beyond equity to foster an inclusive approach to leadership. Even the most generous of people tend to attach judgment to the worthiness or deservingness of the recipients of their benevolence. They are not saints by any means, but they strive to extend non-judgmental benevolence. They understand that all of us can be driven by primal emotions but also recognize that people can cultivate the potential for higher-level cognitive capacities for slow thinking and deliberate and mindful engagement. To meet the needs of today and the future, leadership development must then go beyond competency development in the interpersonal realm and include developing more robust and transcendental mental models. Embracing more expansive and broader identity-based mental models is done while incorporating lower-order egocentric and tribal-centric mental models. Expansive leaders are vigilant about one's own contradictions while embracing similar paradoxes in others. People can be transactional with certain groups of people while being prosocial with select groups of others. That is the tribalistic mental model – somewhat like the in-group/out-group behaviors we have witnessed or experienced in organizations ranging from middle school to boardrooms.

Mental Models or Shapeshifters?

Our mental models are not fixed and static nor are they singular. Multiple and sometimes conflicting mental models simultaneously co-inhabit our minds. For example, during the ongoing COVID-19 crisis, leaders are forced to choose between managing economic and public health outcomes. Similarly, social ventures try to balance market and social orientations or socio-tech ventures that try to balance market, technology, and social orientations.[20] Expansive leaders deftly move between the levels in a fluid, mature, and robust manner appropriate to the situation, and appreciate the complex mental models that people hold. For example, consider Paul who is an excellent engineer. He is very good at his work. But one would never find him working late or taking on additional duties unless paid extra. He is the kind who stops working the minute the clock strikes five. You can term his relationship with his workplace as transactional. Such *quid pro quo* over a short period of time is a defining characteristic of the egocentric identity. However, Paul is also a generous member of his community. He volunteers his time at the local animal shelter and organizes voluntary crews to maintain local trails. Those who deal with Paul at work may not recognize him in his neighborhood. Paul can be said to be egocentric/transactional and tribal-centric with an in-group identity and interdependence-centric all at the same time. Like Paul, we all simultaneously hold complex mental models that are contradictory making for messy, irresolvable situation.

Let me share my own personal tribal-oriented behavior. When I used to work in the private sector, I bought the company shares either in the market or through private placement if an opportunity presented itself. I donate every year to the university in which I work at that time. I don't expect that anyone even notices my donations; the sum I donate is appropriate to my personal net worth; the quantum is too insignificant to attract attention from the top. It is just something I do to claim a bit of emotional ownership in the organizations I am affiliated with. It is an example of a tribalistic mental model. Although my donation would probably go further if I were to donate it to an international organization or a non-profit in my country of origin, I choose to make this donation to 'my' organization. It is not a rational decision based on utilitarian logic but an emotional tribal-centered decision. Even though my relationship with the employer is transactional (contract driven), I deliberately invest in the organization to make my relationship a bit broader. At the same time, I am not opposed to negotiating for my personal outcomes within the organization in a very first-circle, egocentric, transactional manner.

Shifts in identity and mental models do not progress in linear fashion. Mental models sometimes move inward towards more restricted models or outward towards more expansive ones in response to external threats, new information, or an epiphany and change of heart. For example, researchers found that macroeconomic conditions affect individual mental models about people's relationship with and responsibility towards the environment.[21] When people's collective identities, compassion, hope, and optimism get triggered, people's mental models tend to move more outward and more expansive. On the other hand, when people's anxiety, insecurity, and divisive identities get triggered, people's mental models tend to regress into narrower, less benevolent, and more selfish ones. The idea is not simply to resolve the identities but rather to understand how our identities shape our mental models and pay attention to how we engage in each moment.

When Mental Models Collide, Power Comes to Play

When exploitative and extractive models collide with the benevolent ones, unfortunately, there are winners and losers. And usually the winners are those who operate with exploitative mental models. This is because the interdependence-centric, benevolent mental models do not recognize the boundaries between systems and view the entire universe as an interconnected whole, thus leaving those communities defenseless and vulnerable for exploitation. For example, indigenous groups are forced to switch their mode of engagement to the transactional norms of profit sharing in their dealings with private corporations who try to appropriate traditional and indigenous knowledge for commercial exploitation.[22] When these communities find themselves powerless to stop the private corporations who steal their ethnobotanical knowledge but have the support of the private property laws as against the 'commons' knowledge that either belonged to all of humanity or to a specific tribe, they tend to lose.[23] One way for them to avoid being the loser is to establish boundaries and fight for their rights and/or engage in a transactional arrangement such as profit-sharing or income-employment generation thus moving from their universal or expansive mental models to tribal and even transactional models.

Even though moving to restore land to indigenous tribes is essential to repair the damage done, it is still operating in the tribal realm, because the effort it to protect the welfare of the tribe and the legitimacy of its ownership of the land or knowledge. For example, I worked with the Botswana Khoisan (two indigenous tribes – pastoral and hunter gatherer) to whom their land ownership rights had been restored in the form of financial compensation (a transactional economic norm), but the community hasn't benefited much in terms of capacity building. Their business partners operating in a transactional level do not contribute to longterm development and well-being of the tribes themselves. On the other hand, some people move to more expansive mental models and transcend their tribal affiliation as in the case of Megan Phelps-Roper who shared her experience of leaving the Westboro Baptist Church in her book, "Unfollow: A memoir of loving and leaving the Westboro Baptist Church." She was part of a very tight knit in-group, the church in which her grandfather was the founder and her mother an important official. She attributes her departure to her disenchantment with the Westboro Baptist Church and their homophobic and anti-Semitic teachings and to a few open-minded individuals on social media who were instrumental in her changing her mind. Such changes of heart require willingness to suspend judgment and engage across the -isms that separate us.

Mindfulness and Mental Models

The question then is whether such identification with all of humanity and the universe at large can be taught. I have found that mindfulness practice is an appropriate approach to cultivate more expansive and interdependence-centric identity systems and mental models. While any positive change from mindfulness practice is a good outcome, my goal is to demonstrate a methodology for applying mindfulness for transformation of perspectives and cultivation of socially mindful mindsets.[24] Through mindfulness practice, we learn to identify our own complex mental models and even shift them through compassion.[25] How we navigate our complex identities and prioritize core identities affects our decisions around resources and engagement. Depending on the primacy of an identity at a given point, we choose to engage in a combination of boundary setting and boundary spanning behaviors. When our actions are grounded in inward-looking identity systems like individual or ego-centered identity, every other relationship we have is transactional and uses an economic model of outcomes-based negotiations. While it is an essential element, say in job contracts, etc., it becomes a barrier to generosity, empathy, and prosocial behavior at other levels. For example, President Trump's *quid pro quo* with the Ukrainian President is a classic example of not knowing when it is inappropriate, anti-social or even illegal to make that type of deal for personal benefit. On the other hand, a person who is enmeshed in the interpersonal identity of someone – say a colleague, partner, parent, or child – also faces the danger of not honoring their own personal self and core identity. Leadership is a messy affair riled with mistakes, striving up and slipping down, all the while asking ourselves primary questions about who we are, who we wish to be, and how we desire to act. Therefore, this is not a linear progressive model in which a participant proceeds through steps 1 through 5 to arrive at the hallowed halls of great leaders. By living mindfully, we are alive in the moment and to the possibilities that moment offers. I am writing this book stuck in the pandemic-driven quarantine and fueled by the energy of the Black Lives Matter movement. In this historic moment, one can ignore the significance of the moment stuck in the quarantine loop or pay diligent attention to the possibilities it offers. To be alive, one needs to breathe. To be alive to possibilities and respond to them robustly, one needs to be alert, attentive, reflexive, and resilient. Mindfulness practice helps us meet the present moment, any moment, with grace, strength, and resilience.

To do: Mindful Attention to Shifts in Mindsets

Think of a time when you changed your mind about a person or situation recently. What prompted the shift? Did you obtain new information about the person or situation? Or was it something else extraneous to the situation that prompted the change? What did you gain by the shift? What did you lose?

Notes

1 Poonamallee, L. C., & Goltz, S. M. (2014). Beyond Social Exchange Theory: an Integrative Look at Transcendent Mental Models for Engagement. *Integral Theory*, 10(1), 63–90.
2 Sedikides, C., Gaertner, L., & O'Mara, E. M. (2011). Individual Self, Relational Self, Collective Self: Hierarchical Ordering of the Tripartite Self. *Psychological Studies*, 56, 98–107. doi:10.1007/s12646-011-0059-0.
3 Henry, K. B., Arrow, H., & Carini, B. (1999). A Tripartite Model of Group Identification: Theory and Measurement. *Small Group Research*, 30(5), 558–581. doi:10.1177/104649649903000504.
4 Monroe, K. (1996). *The Heart of Altruism: Perceptions of a common humanity.* Princeton, NJ: Princeton University Press.
5 Athukorloa, P. & Resosudarmo, B. (2005). The Indian Ocean Tsunami: Economic Impact, Disaster Management and Lessons. *Australian National University, Economics RSPAS, Departmental Working Papers.* doi:10.1162/153535105776249863.
6 Slove, D., & Zwi, A. B. (2005). Translating compassion into psychosocial aid after the tsunami. *The Lancet*, 365.
7 McFarland, S., Brown, D., & Webb, M. (2013). Identification With All Humanity as a Moral Concept and Psychological Construct. *Current Directions in Psychological Science*, 22(3), 194–198. doi:10.1177/0963721412471346.
8 Crimston, D., Hornsey, M. J., Bain, P. G., & Bastian, B. (2018). Moral expansiveness short form: Validity and reliability of the MESx. *PLOS ONE*, 13(10), e0205373. doi:10.1371/journal.pone.0205373.
9 Crimston, D., Hornsey, M. J., Bain, P. G., & Bastian, B. (2018). Toward a Psychology of Moral Expansiveness. *Current Directions in Psychological Science*, 27(1), 14–19. doi:10.1177/0963721417730888.

10 McFarland, S., Webb, M., & Brown, D. (2012). All humanity is my ingroup: A measure and studies of identification with all humanity. *Journal of Personality and Social Psychology*, 103(5), 830–853. doi:10.1037/a0028724.

11 Pratto, F., & Glasford, D. E. (2008). Ethnocentrism and the value of a human life. *Journal of Personality and Social Psychology*, 95(6), 1411–1428. doi:10.1037/a0012636.

12 Sidanius, J., Pratto, F., & Mitchell, M. (1994). In-Group Identification, Social Dominance Orientation, and Differential Intergroup Social Allocation. *The Journal of Social Psychology*, 134(2), 151–167. doi:10.1080/00224545.1994.9711378.

13 Hale, C. L., & Delia, J. G. (1976). Cognitive complexity and social perspective-taking. *Communication Monographs*, 43(3), 195–203. doi:10.1080/03637757609375932.

14 Groves, K. S., & LaRocca, M. A. (2011). An Empirical Study of Leader Ethical Values, Transformational and Transactional Leadership, and Follower Attitudes Toward Corporate Social Responsibility. *Journal of Business Ethics*, 103, 511–528. doi:10.1007/s10551-011-0877-y.

15 Chrobot-Mason, D., Gerbasi, A., & Cullen-Lester, K. L. (2016). Predicting leadership relationships: The importance of collective identity. *The Leadership Quarterly*, 27(2), 298–311. doi:10.1016/j.leaqua.2016.02.003.

16 Cova, B., & Cova, V. (2002). Tribal Marketing: the tribalization of society and its impact on the conduct of marketing. *European Journal of Marketing*, 36(5/6), 595–620.

17 Nowak, M. A., McAvoy, A., Allen, B., & Wilson, E. O. (2017). The genera form of Hamilton's rule makes no predictions and cannot be tested empirically. *Proceedings of the National Academy of Sciences*, 114(22), 5665–5670. doi:10.1073/pnas.1701805114.

18 Kennett, D. J., Winterhalder, B., Bartruff, J., & Erlandson, J. M. (2009). An ecological model for the emergence of institutionalized social hierarchies on California's Northern Channel Islands. In S. Shennan (Ed.) *Pattern and Process in Cultural Evolution* (pp. 297–314). Berkley, CA: University of California Press.

19 Bergstrom, T. C. (1995). On the evolution of altruistic ethical rules for sibling. *American Economic Review*, 8, 58–79.

20 Poonamallee, L., Scillitoe, J. L., & Joy, S. (2020). *Socio-tech Innovation: Harnessing Technology to serve Social Good*. New York, NY: Palgrave MacMillan.

21 Conroy, S. J., & Emerson, T. L. (2004). Business Ethics and Religion: Religiosity as a Predictor of Ethical Awareness Among Students. *Journal of Business Ethics*, 50, 383–396. doi:10.1023/B:BUSI.0000025040.41263.09.

22 Orozco, D., & Poonamallee, L. C. (2014). The Role of Ethics in the Commercialization of Traditional Knowledge. *Journal of Business Ethics*, 119(2), 275.

23 Poonamallee, L., Joy, S. & Scillitoe, J. (2018). Social as institutional change: Interplay of actors' logic strategies and resources. USC Social Entrepreneurship Conference.

24 Van Doesum, N. J., Van Lange, D. A. W., & Van Lange, P. A. M. (2013). Social mindfulness: Skill and will to navigate the social world. *Journal of Personality and Social Psychology*, 105(1), 86–103. doi:10.1037/a0032540.

25 Condon, P., Desbordes, G., Miller, W. B., & DeSteno, D. (2013). Meditation Increases Compassionate Responses to Suffering. *Psychological Science*, 24(10), 2125–2127. doi:10.1177/0956797613485603.

Part 2

Practice Principles

Chapter 4

Kindness and Curiosity

My goal is to demystify mindfulness practice in the context of helping people cultivate a sense of connectedness to others and an enveloping loving kindness towards all beings in the universe. We cannot get there without adopting kindness as the first practice principle. Along with kindness, I also invite you to bring a playful curiosity to the practice. Most of us assume that for mindfulness and meditation to be serious, it needs to be humorless. As one of the participant reports indicates in Chapter 5, it is a great end if our practice helps us cultivate enough detachment to bring humor to our own monkey selves. Framing the experience of meditation using a competitive, control-centered, ego-driven mental model is not beneficial to cultivating our practice. This leads to us feeling less than others (Who are those mythical others who are so much better than us at everything?) and hence insecure about our own practice. "Am I doing it right?" we ask. When feeling insecure or threatened about our sense of self and identity, we know (and research shows) that it is difficult to develop compassion for oneself let alone others or tap into our more expansive mental models. I find that framing the practice around kindness, curiosity, and gentleness eases the anxiety of the participants and ourselves. Phrases such as "bring your gentle attention, bring your kind attention to the thought or emotion that you are experiencing, bring a gentle curiosity to your breath/body/thought" are reminders to acknowledge the intruder with curiosity and develop kindness towards oneself instead of beating ourselves up for not doing it right. The benefits of loving kindness meditation on generative positive emotions, cultivating connection, and love towards others and oneself is well-documented in literature. Positive emotions broaden our attention, our sense of oneness with our people and our trust in others. Let's look at why it helps to anchor this practice in kindness and curiosity. To do that, I must get a bit technical and talk about how our brain works.

> **Cheat Sheet About Our Sneaky Brain**
>
> - It is the only organ that can look at itself – in mind's eye.
> - It is lazy, efficiency-seeking, and energy-minimizing.
> - Amygdala Vs Prefrontal cortex – Systems 1 and 2 Thinking.
> - It is not so smart – we feel before we think.
> - Cortical thickness determines cognitive complexity.
> - It responds to negative and positive emotional attractors differently.
> - We can teach an old dog new tricks – neuroplasticity.
> - Mirror Neurons, Attunement, and Attachment – Mindsight.

Scientists have made a lot of progress on explaining on how brain works if not the why. For our discussion, I wish to highlight few key insights.

Neuroplasticity. It is uniformly agreed that our brains can learn and grow due to two biological characteristics: neuroplasticity and neurogenesis. Neuroplasticity is the ability to form new connections and pathways between neurons.[1] Neurogenesis is the ability to form new neurons.[2] I have researched how to modify personality traits through an app-based developmental intervention to increase emotional and social intelligence.[3] Through intentional practices such as mindfulness meditation and cognitive behavioral therapy, we can change how we engage with the world. Cognitive training can even reverse brain aging.[4] Exercise and physical activity can slow aging.[5] We can train our brain to slow down, be fast, respond to and interpret cues differently etc. It is true that we can make it by faking it.

Obsessed much or Insightful? Our brain is an interesting organ, as in it can observe its own contents. The self-referential capability of our brain sits in the part called the cortical midline structures. It is considered the core of our self since they connect to every functional domain of our lives.[6] This is good and bad. When our overactive limbic system (bottom-up/ emotional processing) tags negative emotions to our experience, it is a vicious cycle of self-criticism and depression. A very similar vicious cycle results when a top-down (cognitive) failure occurs. We are unable to regulate our emotions and tend to ruminate in them.[7] We discuss more about the top-down and bottom-up processes in the following chapters. In sum, we must focus on kindness when cultivating mindfulness practice. The good news is that when we observe ourselves mindfully, we can also develop insight.

Lazy or Smart? Do you struggle with following an exercise routine? You are not alone. Our brain is wired for minimizing energy expenditure. Scientists call it the physical activity paradox.[8] When there is a conflict between our rational self ("exercising is good for my health") and affect ("ah, I don't want to do it," or "it is going to hurt so much afterwards," etc.), our affect controls the brain much more easily than our top-down process. Our brain's lazy smart ability to minimize energy expenditure also shapes how we sometimes interact with people. Stranger danger is one such irrational behavior.[9] Even though most danger to children is posed by those known to them, generations of children have been taught to fear the stranger. Those who look like us or come from similar backgrounds are assumed to be better fit for a job because there is no translation required. By being over smart, sometimes our brain undercuts our thinking process.

System 1 and System 2 Thinking. Daniel Kahneman wrote the best-seller "Thinking, Fast and Slow"[10] on this topic. System 1 is the Fast-Thinking process by which our very lazy smart and efficient brain processes information, spending a minimal amount of energy and thinking. I remember the first weeks of becoming a first-time mother and being so careful when I changed a diaper. It was a new activity to me. So, like a little child oh so intent on writing those first letters, in those sleep deprived days, I was anxious and careful, gingerly picking the tabs on the side, trying to be careful not to make a mess or hurt the baby in some way. In short order, I became a pro – changing the diaper with one hand while chatting on the phone with the other or while reading something on my computer and tossing the dirty one in the basket in the corner of the room like I was Lebron James. By simply repeating some things more often, we become better at them. By asking someone to repeat some things more often, we can help them become more competent at those things. Our brain is pretty good at that. But, if a friend who had come to help me that afternoon with my baby moved the diaper bin closer to the bed thinking they were being helpful, it would lead to my staying up all night cleaning the mess. So, if we need to move from reacting by rote to responding, we need to train our brains to be willing to work harder and, more importantly, with a beginner's mindset.[11] Mindfulness practice helps us cultivate a beginner's mindset.

Amygdala Vs Prefrontal Cortex.[12] Our limbic system consisting of the amygdala and the hippocampus control our instinctive or rote reaction. They are emotionally charged and depend on stored memories and evolutionary reactions. Whereas our prefrontal cortex is the seat of our rationality. Combined with the fact that our brain is actually not that smart – as in we feel before we think[13] – it is not a surprise that we find it very difficult to process new information (such as "oh, they may be a different tribe, but they may be good people too"), regulate our emotions ("oh my god, it is just my luck that I always get the middle seat on the plane – no it is irrational, perhaps I buy my tickets late or don't want to pay the additional fees incurred for obtaining an aisle seat") and anything that requires slowing our minds and thinking more carefully and mindfully.

Mirror Mirror Look At Me. A saving grace of our brains is that we are truly wired for connection. We are so moved by empathy and compassion because our brain has mirror neurons.[14] We are biologically wired to connect and mirror other people's emotions. Larry Stevens and Woodruff's edited volume,[15] "The Neuroscience of Empathy, Compassion, and Self-compassion," is an excellent handbook on the three inter-related domains. Daniel Siegel's work on attunement and mindsight[16] presents a psychological perspective using mindfulness and attachment theory. It explains why the usually pacific Canadians surprise us by breaking store windows and rioting when their hockey team loses. Emotions are contagious.[17] We react to other people's emotions.

Positive and Negative Emotional Attractors. Emotions are not only contagious. Our brains' ability to learn, change, and grow (neuroplasticity) is related to whether our brains get activated by negative or positive emotions.[18] One of my favorite professors from graduate school, Dr. Richard Boyatzis, has done a lot of work on this front in the context of coaching. He calls coaching to the Positive Emotional Attractors (PEA) as Coaching with Compassion and Negative Emotional Attractors (NEA) as Coaching for Compliance. Research has shown that PEA engagement allows people to be open, and triggers the parasympathetic nervous system, default mode network and positive emotions allowing us to feel safe, be open to others, possibilities and learning and growth.[19] [20] On the other hand, NEA engages the sympathetic stress system, increases self-consciousness, engages a defensive posture leading to the shutting down of our openness to change, reducing our flexibility and increasing our cognitive rigidity.

Mindfulness beginning can be exhilarating but also frustrating. Some of us go step a forward and start looking at mindfulness success as another goal we must accomplish for the day. Some of us even want to be the best at contemplative practice. We address these competitive, instrumental tendencies by being kind and curious. Curiosity allows us to notice our own internal processes. Kindness allows us to be non-judgmental about them. A novice participant writes:

> As I was going through my mindfulness exercises each day, I struggled with maintaining my attention and presence. My mind kept wandering and I was getting frustrated at myself. During Latha's facilitative meditation, she mentioned that the listener must show themselves compassion. If your mind wanders, it's okay. Knowing it was okay and I wasn't "doing it wrong" or something was wrong with me for not being able to stay present, I kept going and didn't give up trying. It made me realize that meditation is not so much listening to yourself breathing and not letting thoughts in your head, and more about forgiving yourself if they do.

Practicing mindfulness is supposed to reduce anxiety, not increase it. Mindfulness practice is not a race to the top. As Lily Tomlin once was supposed to have famously said, "The trouble with the rat race is that even if you win, you are still a rat." No point in chanting and dancing while still stuck in a rat race. A successful mid-career professional at the end of the program wrote about what he learned about the ego:

> Throughout this final week, I've been thinking a lot about the ego ... specifically, my ego. I believe the most profound, useful thing I've learned from this semester, or become aware of, is that I have been living in my head for the last 8+ years. I have been living in my mind and not following my heart, or rather, not following my joy and feeling that joy in my heart ... in my body. I have thought about joy and have definitely felt joy, but largely found this joy out of my thoughts/feelings and not my body/heart. In our Loving Kindness guided meditation this week, the prompt that stood out to me the most was: "Look at yourself from the eyes of someone who loves you ..." This really struck me. It took me outside of the idea of who I should or should not be in order to be loved ... It made me start thinking about all the things that I told myself I needed to do, say, feel, think (or not do, say, feel, think) in order to be my best self, a self that people will love me for, a self that will achieve and be ambitious and be successful and respected by all ... All of this is my ego. It was amazing all of the great, positive things I thought about myself when I put myself in the shoes of my partner and why she loves me for exactly who I am – and her love has nothing to do with the bullshit idea of who I think I should be, or the ego I have constructed for myself.

To do: Kindness Exercise

Think of an experience that was unpleasant or uncomfortable (e.g., trying some new food or feeling sick) or made you feel tired. Write a brief paragraph about the feelings and emotions you felt during that time. Pay attention to your sensations and emotions with compassion. Make an aspiration to be kind to your suffering with self-care and compassion.

Notes

1 Shaffer, J. (2016). Neuroplasticity and Clinical Practice: Building Brain Power for Health. *Frontiers in psychology*, 7, 1118. doi:10.3389/fpsyg.2016.01118.
2 Ming, G. L., & Song, H. (2011). Adult neurogenesis in the mammalian brain: significant answers and significant questions. *Neuron*, 70(4), 687–702. doi:10.1016/j.neuron.2011.05.001.
3 Poonamallee, L., Harrington, A., Nagpal, M., & Musial, A. (2018). Improving Emotional Intelligence through Personality Development: The Effect of the Smartphone App based Dharma Life Program on Emotional Intelligence. *Frontiers in Psychology*, 9, 169. doi:10.3389/fpsyg.2018.00169.

4 Park, D. C., & Bischof, G. N. (2013). The aging mind: neuroplasticity in response to cognitive training. *Dialogues in clinical neuroscience*, 15(1), 109–119.

5 Ahlskog, J. E., Geda, Y. E., Graff-Radford, N. R., & Petersen, R. C. (2011). Physical exercise as a preventive or disease-modifying treatment of dementia and brain aging. *Mayo Clinic proceedings*, 86(9), 876–884. doi:10.4065/mcp.2011.0252.

6 Nejad, A. B., Fossati, P., & Lemogne, C. (2013). Self-referential processing, rumination, and cortical midline structures in major depression. *Frontiers in human neuroscience*, 7, 666. doi:10.3389/fnhum.2013.00666.

7 Sparks, S., Moodie, R., & Kritikos, A. (2016). Top-down control and directed attention in self-reference effects: Goal-directed movements and the SAN. *Cognitive Neuroscience*, 7(1–4), 25–27. doi:10.1080/17588928.2015.1075488.

8 Holtermann, A., Krause, N., Beek, A., & Straker, L. (2017). The physical activity paradox: six reasons why occupational physical activity (OPA) does not confer the cardiovascular health benefits that leisure time physical activity does. *British Journal of Sports Medicine*, 52. doi:10.1136/bjsports-2017–097965.

9 Wodda, A. (2018). Stranger Danger! *Journal of Family Strengths*, 18(1), Article 3. Available at https://digitalcommons.library.tmc.edu/jfs/vol18/iss1/3.

10 Kahneman, D. (2011). *Thinking, Fast and Slow*. New York, NY: Farrar, Straus and Giroux.

11 Younie, L. (2017). Beginner's mind. *London journal of primary care*, 9(6), 83–85. doi:10.1080/17571472.2017.1370768.

12 Park, A. T., Leonard, J. A., Saxler, P. K., Cyr, A. B., Gabrieli, J., & Mackey, A. P. (2018). Amygdala-medial prefrontal cortex connectivity relates to stress and mental health in early childhood. *Social cognitive and affective neuroscience*, 13 (4), 430–439. doi:10.1093/scan/nsy017.

13 Oosterwijk, S., Lindquist, K. A., Anderson, E., Dautoff, R., Moriguchi, Y., & Barrett, L. F. (2012). States of mind: emotions, body feelings, and thoughts share distributed neural networks. *NeuroImage*, 62(3), 2110–2128. doi:10.1016/j.neuroimage.2012.05.079.

14 Acharya, S., & Shukla, S. (2012). Mirror neurons: Enigma of the metaphysical modular brain. *Journal of natural science, biology, and medicine*, 3(2), 118–124. doi:10.4103/0976-9668.101878.

15 Stevens, L., & Woodruff, C. (2018). The neuroscience of empathy, compassion, and self-compassion. San Diego, CA: Elsevier.

16 Siegel, D. J. (2010). *Mindsight: The new science of personal transformation*. New York, NY: Bantam Books.

17 Kramer, A. D. I., Guillory, J. E., & Hancock, J. T. (2014). Emotional contagion through social networks *Proceedings of the National Academy of Sciences*, 111 (24), 8788–8790. doi:10.1073/pnas.1320040111.

18 Boyatzis, R. E., Rochford, K., & Taylor, S. N. (2015). The role of the positive emotional attractor in vision and shared vision: toward effective leadership, relationships, and engagement. *Frontiers in psychology*, 6, 670. doi:10.3389/fpsyg.2015.00670.

19 Howard, A. R. (2015). Coaching to vision versus coaching to improvement needs: a preliminary investigation on the differential impacts of fostering positive and negative emotion during real time executive coaching sessions. *Frontiers in Psychology*, 6, 455. doi:10.3389/fpsyg.2015.00455.

20 Howard, A. (2006). Positive and negative emotional attractors and intentional change. *Journal of Management Development*, 25, 657–670. doi:10.1108/02621710610678472.

Chapter 5

Instrumentality to Transformation

My goal is to help transcend (and include) the instrumentality of personal empowerment at an individual level and move towards social mindfulness and expansive leadership for transformative outcomes, specifically in developing a strong sense of connection to others and helping in bridging the -isms in our polarized world. Much of the emphasis of secular mindfulness so far has been on instrumental outcomes (such as stress reduction or productivity increases) through practicing mindfulness in the worlds of work, health, and education. There is enough strong evidence to support the implementation of mindfulness practice for improving these outcomes. My own research finds that mindfulness practice increases emotional and social intelligence and prosocial orientation. Mindfulness reduces aging, increases performance in standardized tests, and improves employee outcomes such as work engagement and job performance. Secular adoption (that I support very much) has sanitized and obscured the spiritual roots and goals of meditation and mindfulness practice. The goal of most meditation and mindfulness practice across religions, and especially in the eastern traditions is transcendence, i.e. heightened awareness and interconnectivity[1] and develop a mindful self.[2] However, most mindfulness practitioners and teachers in the secular world haven't found a way to connect to or call for that, especially in the context of workplace implementation. On the one hand, this approach makes complete sense because of the religious connotations of mindfulness practice that do not belong at the workplace. On the other hand, when the original intent is ignored, the potential impact of practice gets truncated. These corporate and rationality-based accounts gloss over spiritual aspects of the practice and the struggle that accompanies self-realization and uncovering our complex inner worlds. If people experience what is possible – oneness and dissolution of division of boundaries – through this practice, then it becomes difficult to stoke the competitive rivalries that are fueled by tribal identities in the interest of preserving market superiority, profit maximizing outcomes, and the business of war. Mindfulness does not always lead to this as can be seen in the genocides in Sri Lanka and Myanmar led by Buddhist monks.

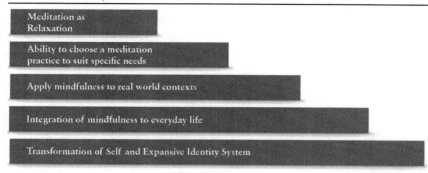

Figure 5.1 Stages of Development of Mindful Awareness

However, the starting point is almost always individual and personal well-being for most people. Without deliberate intent they may never progress beyond that stage in their practice. Mindfulness becomes mindless. The proposed practice model in this book has been tested and refined to go beyond the instrumental and facilitate personal transformation towards being an expansive leader. The figure provides an insight into the development possible through mindfulness practice.

Mindfulness as Relaxation. Most people come to the practice to seek relaxation or reduce anxiety. For example, one of the participants in the program writes about using mindfulness practice to reduce anxiety during a turbulent transcontinental flight. This is a useful but instrumental end to the practice.

> It was a 14-hour direct flight to Dubai, and I was super worried about how I would manage to be seated for that long. The flight took off and my journey went on smooth until we hit terrible air turbulence over a massive body of water. I was asleep, but the turbulence woke me up. Not just me, but it evoked in each passenger a slight bit of panic. That is when I shut my eyes, folded my legs, and tried remaining as calm as I could be. By this time, I had stopped watching any show or even listening to music and was just focusing on how I could possibly get past the situation. I managed to zone out all the chaos of the background and remain still for a considerable time. Minutes later, when I opened my eyes, I had realized that I had successfully overcome the moment of anxiety and felt relaxed after.

Another participant writes about the benefits they derive in terms of more focus.

Since the beginning of this class when I started using meditation, I have found that I have been able to achieve more focus and tend to indulge in the benefits of meditation rather than just sitting and thinking about anything that comes to mind.

Mindfulness as Agency. The program cycles participants through various types of meditation such as breath, body scan, drawing, walking, thoughts, emotions, loving kindness, and specific emotions such as gratitude, etc. Familiarity with the different types and experiential understanding allows the practitioner to move to self-empowerment where they choose the style of meditation that suits their particular need at any given time. For example, some may choose to focus on gratitude when they are particularly facing a challenging situation. Some may choose body scan when they struggle to fall asleep. I strongly support and encourage participants to use different apps and unguided meditation bells, etc. to deepen their sense of agency around their practice during and beyond the program. For example, one participant writes:

> After the first gratitude meditation, later in the week I returned for a silent meditation focusing on my gratitude for my five senses specifically. Not only did this meditation seem to ground me, it also opened me to areas that I had taken for granted. I'd like to further explore this type of meditation in the future, focusing on just one sense for the entirety of the twenty minutes. I feel like that would take a lot of concentration and I feel like I need to work up to it.

Not only does she feel empowered to choose a different meditation but also devises her own variation that allowed her to go safely and bravely to areas that she had taken for granted. She is reflexive and understands that the next step that she wants to take may take more from her, but she will know when she is ready.

Another participant writes:

> My experience in the class in this last third of the semester has been great. I love how open your classroom is; this allows me to feel freely about speaking my mind and having an opinion. I am pleased with the continuation of practicing mindful meditation in your classroom and while being at home.

My teaching style did not change over the period. But his experience and sense of agency in the classroom changed where he felt safe and empowered to claim his own voice and space.

Mindfulness as Mobility. I find that participants tend to then move to where they begin feeling comfortable applying mindfulness to real world contexts. For example, one participant writes about her relationship with a roommate.

> I did notice that a relationship with one of my housemates has shifted a bit over the last couple of weeks. I don't think she has even noticed, but my attitude and internal processing about the way she engages with me have changed ever so slightly. I am more able to think about her actions, and my reactions, in a bit more neutral way, instead of getting mad and responding to her from a place of anger and frustration.

This is a deliberate effort at applying the mindfulness learning and practice to a challenging real-world situation. Read this account by another participant:

> Earlier tonight, after picking up my kids, I finally found a parking spot in front of my house and was about to pull in when a fire truck pulled up behind me, forcing me to drive around the block and lose my spot, as a result. I completely lost my temper. It is moments like these – when an extremely frustrating event happens – that I fall into the temper tantrum problem that I learned from watching my father all those years. I calmed down by deep breathing, but I was upset with myself for having the moment of extreme anger and allowing it to overtake me. For something as silly as a parking spot ... I actually found a mindfulness challenge video on mindful commuting. It challenges you to be mindful anytime that you travel. Perhaps this is something I can be more deliberate about. It is called "Eliminate Road Rage!" I have done so much better not getting frustrated by public transportation, but when I have two kids in the car and it's bedtime and one has already fallen asleep and I have four bags and a two-year old to carry, I apparently do not like losing my parking spot!

Not only was she able to call on herself to be calm by deep breathing at a stressful moment but she then observed herself in that moment of extreme emotion, chose another mindful activity to help her with what she finds most stressful – commuting with two young children in New York City – and finally ends her own journal with humor!

Mindfulness as commitment. This step is making a commitment to live a mindful life. Most people who have experienced the positive effects of mindfulness know that it is useful and healing. But most people also drop it in crunch time when they need it the most. Some may build in time for practice on an everyday basis. Or they begin and maintain a daily journaling practice. End of the day journaling is an act of bravery and commitment when most of us feel depleted and don't even have the energy to wash our faces let alone face a journal. At this stage, practice is not an afterthought but an anchor and punctuation to their everyday life. A participant writes about preparing for life after the program.

> I'm so happy that this practice has also been integrated into my home and that my partner is taking part in meditation and mindfulness practices to assist him in relaxing as well as with his anxiety. This has been a wonderful learning experience. This week I took the opportunity to continue my morning ritual of tea and meditation and I am continuing to look at it as an experience in life as something I have to do. If I'm able to do it, it provides me some peace in the morning and assists me in being in a better mood throughout the day. Night-time meditation has always been the best type of meditation for me as it really helps me fall asleep and feel relaxed right before bed and is a practice that my partner also really enjoys doing as well. Keeping the meditation Journal has also been a wonderful experience. It has allowed me to reflect on my day today as well as on how I'm feeling that day and how I felt while completing the meditation. This week I focus a lot on meditating and staying relaxed as right now my anxiety is a little bit high because I am busy planning my mom's 60th birthday party, working on a very important project at work, and of course trying to keep up with schoolwork as well. I really was using my meditation this week to take some time for myself and the mindfulness practices assisted me in taking those moments that I needed. This has been a great Journey and I'm very appreciative of the things that I learned during this course.

This practice is a gift that keeps on giving. For example, she continues to acknowledge the benefit of relaxation. But she also talks about using her meditation to take some time for herself – there's your empowerment. She chooses her meditation styles based on what works for her. She has integrated into a ritual some morning tea. She has brought the practice to include her spouse. It is not separate from her life. She talks about her mother's birthday, schoolwork, personal life, and work life in her journal on her practice. That is a mindful life.

Mindfulness as transformation. At its roots, mindfulness practice is not just about being more productive in the pragmatic realm. It is about connecting with the vast sacred universe and feeling that connection from the tip of our toes to the top of our heads. Feeling that oneness with the universe is the sacred knowledge experienced and embodied in every fiber, every cell; when one feels the heart swell with the connection and gratitude for the moment. The very first time I felt it was in the desert. I spent all evening watching the sun go down from across the dunes. Then, I turned around to watch the moon rise from the east. I felt at one with the sand, sun, moon, and the earth and everything in it. One doesn't need to go away to the desert for that experience. It can even happen in New York City. One morning when I was walking my dog in the Randall's/Wards Islands in New York City, I recalled how Wards Island had been the site to which the city had relocated remains of hundreds of thousands of people from Madison Square and Bryant Park graveyards. I felt a shiver deep into my bones. I sent a silent thank you to all those folks who were before me in my city, a place to which I feel deeply connected. The city, its past and present, from the Lenape people (the first inhabitants) to today's brunch crowd, suffused my being. Mindfulness practice provides that opportunity for feeling that connection to the universe. Tragically, not too long after that, my favorite place for my morning walk also became an overflow morgue during the peak of COVID-19 in New York City. In my heart, I suffered with all the families that lost their loved ones. Transformative practice strengthens but also softens. It is life itself.

Consider this participant, an Executive Director of a non-profit who writes about her experience hinting at moving from personal stress management to becoming a better leader through compassion.

> While my stress has never manifested in an abuse of power or lack of compassion or empathy for my employees, it has diminished my hope and ability to attend to myself, which can be frustrating and discouraging for my employees. Practicing mindfulness meditation deliberately, through the help of this course and in other aspects of my life, will allow me to cultivate the self-awareness and self-compassion that will allow me to be a better leader and role model to those around me. I have always thought of my job as a supervisor as more of a "coaching" job, as the reading suggests. My leadership style has always been to engage people to reach their true potential. Where I have missed the mark, I believe, is in extending those practices to myself and leading by example. I can already see how deliberately practicing meditative practices daily leads to self-love, self-awareness, and compassion, and I look forward to seeing its effect on my leadership style as I embark on this new role.

A young female activist who participated in the program writes:

> Many of the shifts of my mind and body throughout my life were due to a form of survival and instincts, rather than a choice. It wasn't a choice for me to grow up too quick, take responsibilities at a young age, and have to develop such an "old" mentality as a younger age. [It] was due to the circumstances around me and the things I had to face. This time, this class challenged me into taking this "survival" instinct and having control over it, rather than it, controlling me. I was able to

do something that was so difficult for me (meditating) and use it to heal rather than "survive."

My goal is to reclaim the sacredness of this practice and foster more inclusive, interdependence-centric mental models and identity systems. In the eastern traditions, wisdom and compassion go together. Seeing the many in one and one in many. One cannot be wiser without feeling a broader, expansive, and intersectional identity that is intertwined with the universe at large. One cannot be wise and not be compassionate. One in Many and Many in One. We are all one.

G, who used to become very frustrated during initial practice, wrote this after eight weeks of consistent practice and in the middle of COVID-19 lockdown:

> This afternoon I went through the gratitude, love, and kindness mediation you sent last week Latha (thank you!). What I realized that even though events are canceled, being in an office space is canceled, classes are canceled (momentarily) there are so many things that COVID-19 has not canceled. Love, music, dancing, progress, meditation, dreaming, self-care, reading, having fun, walking in nature, calling friends/family, practicing gratitude, and staying optimistic.

How do we create a transformative experience? By intentionally and mindfully letting the practice lead and getting out of the way. By letting the practice do its magic. Imagine growing a plant that needs support. Practice is the ground, it is the sun, light and water, and it is also the trellis that will support your plant to grow strong and flexible reaching for the sky. To cultivate is to grow something intentionally. In this approach, we grow our practice and by which we grow more expansive mental models and allow ourselves to be transformed.

To do: Epiphany Exercise

Think of a recent time when you had an aha moment. It could be as simple as learning that fennel seeds add sparkle to pasta sauce to a momentous discovery about yourself or someone close to you.

What made that moment stand out? Did anyone facilitate that aha moment? How did that change your life?

Notes

1 Trammel, R. C. (2017). Tracing the roots of mindfulness: Transcendence in Buddhism and Christianity. *Journal of Religion & Spirituality in Social Work: Social Thought*, 36(3), 367–383. doi:10.1080/15426432.2017.1295822.
2 Xiao, Q., Yue, C., He, W., & Yu, J. Y. (2017). The Mindful Self: A Mindfulness-Enlightened Self-view. *Frontiers in psychology*, 8, 1752. doi:10.3389/fpsyg.2017.01752.

Chapter 6

Holistic: Top-Down and Bottom-up Engagement

The third key principle undergirding this model is a holistic top-down and bottom-up engagement.[1] In this chapter, we build on the previous chapter's neuroscience primer. We are going to examine how our emotions and mental models are generated. To remind ourselves, mental models are a set of assumptions, values, frames, and beliefs we have about a situation or the world that shapes how we connect with other people, other living beings, and the universe at large. Through mindfulness practice, we are attempting to move our mental models to be more expansive and foster a connectedness with the universe, thus reducing the impact of tribal and other divisive identities. We keep in mind a deeper awareness of our identities and mental models and the complexity of human engagement.

We form our mental models through a combination of and interaction between top-down process, i.e. cognitive framing, and bottom-up process or affective arousal. Bottom-up process is emotional arousal that affects how we react to a situation. If empathy is aroused, people tend to be prosocial, giving, and generous. For example, when we see a commercial about a disaster or a refugee settlement and our empathy gets aroused, we donate to the International Rescue Committee or International Red Cross or other such humanitarian relief organizations. On the other hand, if fear or insecurity is aroused by a stimulus, people tend to focus more on their own needs than others' needs. For example, when refugees or undocumented immigrants are perceived as a threat to one's own employment or a danger to the community, people tend to respond negatively. In the brain parlance,[2] bottom-up means processes triggered by the lower-order brain structures such as the amygdala. Top-down on the other hand are mediated by the prefrontal cortex, i.e. through cognitive frames and rational approaches. For example, psychotherapy that focuses on cognitive reappraisals – i.e. rewiring how we perceive, or frame stimuli – is an example of top-down mechanism. Behaviors that are generated by top-down processes are more responsive to cognitive methods that restructure interpretations of the situation. Bottom-up inspired behaviors are more responsive to behavioral reinforcement methods such as positive reinforcement or gamification for exercise or gold stars for students. Behavioral self-regulation and delayed gratification because of the focus on long-term goals is a top-down process. Brain imaging studies also indicate that top-down processes are more enduring than bottom-up processes. That explains why we can see a cute puppy's picture on the shelter website or a picture of a refugee child on a news item, donate instantly, even shed a few tears and then move on with our lives. Bottom-up aroused emotions tend to be more transient. They pass. Feelings are transient. The amygdala is ever present but fleeting. The prefrontal cortex, on the hand, is hard to engage but stubborn and persistent.

More recent research has extended this to examine how mindfulness engages the top-down and bottom-up processes of emotion regulation.[3] One interpretation is that bottom-up mindfulness is associated with reduced activation of the limbic region. When we practice meditation and other mindfulness activities, we slow our reactive lizard brain and that means that limbic region activation is lower. So, we don't jump off the top of a building just because we didn't get the job that we really wanted. We develop some perspective and our response is not disproportionate to the situation. A second take is that mindfulness engages our prefrontal cortex in cognitive reappraisal of the stimulus thus increasing emotional self-regulation. As a reminder, our prefrontal cortex is the slower part of the brain, capable of taking a moment to reflect, think deliberately and slowly to arrive at an appropriate decision. When we don't get the job we really wanted, we engage our thinking brain to examine the experience and learn from it. That detachment and distance from the event (in our mind) also reduces the emotional valence from the pain of rejection. We also learn how to reframe it: "Yeah, it is okay that I didn't get the job. Now I don't have to move at a time that is crucial for my son." Or "I am so grateful that I already have a job that I like, and my colleagues like me. Yes, I would have liked the bigger job, but all in good time." Coming out of an understanding that life is fleeting, flowing, or that things that go up also go down, etc. we automatically engage in emotional reappraisal. The disappointing stimulus hasn't changed. How we perceive them changes.

The mindfulness model laid out in the book engages both top-down and bottom-up mechanisms for shifting mental models. We deliberately cycle through practices that provide opportunities to examine our emotions and affective reactions scaffolded by reflection that privileges non-judgmental awareness. In the bottom-up mode, we engage in more of an open monitoring of the whole experience. In the top-down, we actively reframe and appraise the situation differently to change our perception of how we experience something.

C, a participant, writes thus:

> I experienced a range of feelings through this week's Emotions Meditation (and also began to understand the difference between feelings Vs

emotions). My range of feelings went something like this: calm > happy > anxious > overwhelmed > tired > relieved > overwhelmed again > anxious again > dull/flat > happy again > grateful. As all these emotions passed through me, they were all tied to memories or to-do lists or future worries and obstacles. It wasn't until Latha said in the meditation, "it's not the why, it's the what" that I realized that it was hard for me to name the emotion/feeling without letting my mind wander due to all the associated memories I mentioned above. What I realized is that I feel a much stronger connection to my mind than I do my body (aka I have a stronger connection to my feelings than emotions). I often feel in control of my feelings. I have somewhat mastered the art of convincing myself that certain feelings are okay – they will pass. I generally "feel" happy with myself and the environment I choose (or am lucky to choose in certain cases). What I'm beginning to learn about myself is that there are absolutely some emotions inside of me that I've held deep down and disconnected my mind from. I'm first realizing this because of the disconnect I feel to my body. It's very hard for me to listen to my body and take cues from it – how am I feeling physically, emotionally, mentally ... It's a good feeling to actually make this clarification between my body and emotions Vs my mind and feelings, but now I'm wondering where I even begin to try and detangle my emotions that have been buried in my subconscious my whole life.

Another example shows the reappraisal, top-down response.

One of my biggest challenges was understanding my own emotional state and being able to identify it. For a long time, identifying and naming them was a challenge due to fear of having to confront them, and understanding them. The first time I spoke out loud that I experienced sadness, anxiety, depression, happiness, etc., it became so much easier for me to deeply understand where my emotions were coming from ... Aside from this, after breathing and centering myself, I started to question WHY I was feeling this nervous about something that might seem so minor to others. For me, this thing I am starting on Friday is something that I have always seen myself doing, but that I have never done before ... This fear of the unknown was what was trying to stop me and created these emotional barriers. It was my inner critic trying to protect me from the unknown, from something out of my comfort zone. I realized that I have gotten in situations far beyond this, that have been far more challenging and uncomfortable. I also told myself that feeling like this is okay, but also telling my inner critic that I can handle it, and I don't need any protection, this inner critic that's strictly speaking from fear.

To do: Top-Down/Bottom-up Exercise

- Find a picture in a magazine or book or on the computer and let yourself respond naturally and quickly. What is your emotional response to the image? Makes notes using the following table.
- Now construct a negative interpretation for the image. Make notes.
- Find a second picture and let yourself respond naturally. What is your emotional response to the image?
- Now construct a positive interpretation for the second image.
- How did it feel different to respond naturally and actively construct an interpretation?

Image No	Natural emotional response	Constructed interpretation
1		
2		

What did you learn? How did it feel different to respond naturally and actively constructing an explanation?

Notes

1 Ochsner, K. N., Ray, R. R., Hughes, B., McRae, K., Cooper, J. C., Weber, J., Gabrieli, J. D., & Gross, J. J. (2009). Bottom-up and top-down processes in emotion generation: common and distinct neural mechanisms. *Psychological science*, 20(11), 1322–1331. doi:10.1111/j.1467-9280.2009.02459.x.
2 McRae, K., Misra, S., Prasad, A. K., Pereira, S. C., & Gross, J. J. (2012). Bottom-up and top-down emotion generation: implications for emotion regulation. *Social cognitive and affective neuroscience*, 7(3), 253–262. doi:10.1093/scan/nsq103.
3 Chiesa, A., Serretti, A., & Jakobsen, J. C. (2013). Mindfulness: top-down or bottom-up emotion regulation strategy? *Clinical Psychology Review*, 33(1), 82–96. doi:10.1016/j.cpr.2012.10.006.

Part 3

Know Thyself

Chapter 7

Constructing and Deconstructing Identities

Who am I? How did I get here? Where I am going?

These pivotal existential questions have animated many religious, spiritual, and humanistic traditions for centuries. How we answer these questions determines who we accept as part of our worlds and who we reject, how we allocate resources, how we make decisions, who we share with, who we keep out, how we relate, how we connect, who we appreciate, who we can connect with – all that shapes how we lead. Earlier, we touched upon the 'one human family notion' shared among those non-Jewish people who rescued the Jews during World War II, even putting themselves and their families at risk. Sharing with kin and non-kin is a human trait that predisposes us for cooperation.[1]

For example, an early Indian scripture goes like this:

> Lokah Samastha Sukhino Bhavantu – May all beings everywhere be happy and free, and may the thoughts, words, and actions of my own life contribute in some way to that happiness and to that freedom for all.

These notions of identity are expansive, broad, and inclusive against the narrower tribal or transactional notions of how we define ourselves. If the non-Jews did not think of the Jews in danger as fellow humans, they wouldn't have risked their own families to rescue the 'other.' Social identity explains many of the sharing mechanisms from government[2] to AI based virtual communities.[3] Collective and shared identities foster altruism, cooperation, and prosocial orientation.[4] On the other hand, the tendency to dehumanize others is strongly associated with Social Dominance Orientation and a penchant for hierarchy within groups of people – a tribal orientation of Us Vs Them. It is difficult to imagine people with this orientation to be an inclusive leader. Consider President Trump's response to the Black Lives Matter protests or his lack of acknowledgement of the disproportionate loss of black and brown lives during the Covid-19 pandemic. His characterization of Mexican immigrants as rapists and drug dealers is not dissimilar to the Nazis terming the Jews vermin. Using that kind of language repeatedly, even if simply to appeal to a certain set of people for political ends, is bound to strengthen those perceptions in oneself. This is exacerbated by confirmation bias. We are wired to seek evidence to confirm our truths or beliefs as real. To be one step ahead of our own cognitive biases, we must actively look for evidence that counters our assumptions and beliefs and revisit our identities. We must be vigilant about how we define ourselves and how that shapes our actions and leadership behaviors.

How do we self-define? Do we identify more or less strongly with a particular group? That determines how much our mental models are shaped by that group's values and norms. For example, consider religious affiliation. How religious are we? How did our religion shape us? For some of us, religion gave us the top-down cognitive frames that make up our mental models. For some of us who are Militant/Radical Atheists, our identity was developed in antipathy to organized religion. Teachings of our family religion provide us part of our mental model even though we may have abandoned the religion. Cultural, political, ideological, and professional affiliations along with fundamental demographic characteristics such as race, gender, age, geographic location, and national culture all play a part in our identity creation, maintenance, and change. As an immigrant myself, I am shaped both by my national culture of origin as well as the culture of my adopted country. In the coming chapters, we will look at the different facets of our identities and how they are interlinked.

To do: Who Am I?

- Who am I? Ask this question of yourself at least nine times to unpack your identity. Every time you answer this question iteratively, write your answer down.
- How do these identities overlap?
- Can you rank your identity systems? Alternatively, you can also do this as a Venn diagram or concentric circles to identify overlaps, and connections.
- Think of your most recent important decision or moment. Reflect on what identity systems played a part in how you handled the situation or conflict.
- What did you learn about yourself?

For trainers: This exercise is also very appropriate to try in a dyad/paired situation and groups.

Multi-Dimensional and Interdependent

Expansive leaders have a multi-dimensional understanding of identity system. They understand we all hold membership in different spaces and groups and sometimes these different dimensions interact with each other. That sometimes we are forced to prioritize one dimension versus other depending on the situation, and expansive leaders try to co-hold the various dimensions. Consider the intersectionality between race, gender, and class. Mary Pattillo eloquently writes about the class and lifestyle fractures within the black identity within the persistence of a collective black experience and identity.[5] Expansive leaders appreciate the complexity and nuances of a multi-dimensional identity. The question is not whether one is multi-dimensional or not. The question is only if one is aware of the multiple dimensions that define our identity. For example, consider His Holiness the Dalai Lama's biography on his website.

1   His first identity is that of a human being, encouraging people to be happy, and is committed to supporting the adoption of human or universal or secular values such as warm-heartedness, compassion, forgiveness, etc. among those people, including those who are not religious. Despite him being the leader of a religious sect, he explicitly excludes religiosity as a criterion for who deserves to be happy, demonstrating his lack of tribalism in this aspect.

2   Second, he defines himself as a Buddhist monk and encourages harmony between all religions and explicitly declares that all religions are equally valid. He writes that while the notion of one truth, one religion may be relevant to the individual practitioner, when it comes to the wider community, there is a need to recognize that people practice different religions and there are several aspects to the truths.

3   Third, he defines himself as a Tibetan and a custodian of Tibetan language, heritage, and culture, including Tibet's natural environment.

4   Finally, he presents his commitment to reviving awareness of ancient Indian knowledge among the Indian youth, a nod to his adoptive home in exile since 1959.

Expansive leaders see themselves as part of an interdependent ecosystem. His Tibetan identity does not negate his appreciation of the home India has provided him for more than a half-century. His Buddhist identity does not cancel his acknowledgement of the validity of religious pluralism. Neither his religious identity nor his cultural/geographic identity negates his concern for the humankind at large as a fellow human being.

Let me share how I identify myself at this moment. I am a straight, cis woman of Indian roots, rooted and planted in the US who made a voluntary choice to emigrate here as an adult, and became an American through naturalization, a sole parent, a daughter, wife and partner to a white male, scholar, professor, unschooling mother, New Yorker, socio-tech entrepreneur, a human, a living being that is nourished by and grateful to Mother Earth, lover of books and woods, an advocate for progressive society and someone who is learning how to be anti-racist.

How these notions of identity overlap with each other and in relation to each other is a critical factor in unpacking identity. Our identities are not necessarily static and fixed. Because we are sentient beings and learning machines, our life experience forces us to reassess who we are. We learn new things, experience our own personal aha moments or epiphanies, and redefine our identity as we go along. Awareness of some of these identities grow with understanding and awareness over time.

If I had done this exercise ten years ago, I would not have added terms such as cis, straight, anti-racist as part of my identity definition. These worlds were not part of my vocabulary then. With this expanded self-definition, I am more aware of my own cisgender privilege and my responsibility to respect and protect the dignity of my trans brothers and sisters. You may also notice that I don't define myself in religious or spiritual terms. I am not religious, but I am also not anti-religion, so I don't define my identity in relation to religion in general. But there are other non-believers who are vehemently anti-religion and define themselves thus and their identity is as tied to the notion of religion as those vehemently opposed to it. This exercise helps us uncover our affiliations, who we connect with, who we struggle to accept and connect and learn more about our relational triggers. So, know thyself.

Egocentrism

The kind of leadership we exhibit and inhabit is tied to how we see our own identities in connection with others and how that understanding colors how we make decisions and how we engage with others. When we see ourselves as atomized individuals with no ties, responsibilities, and obligations beyond ourselves, we tend to solely focus on our personal outcome. We overlook or exclude consideration of the impact our decisions may cause to other people, other living beings and the physical environment. This is an egocentric identity. When egocentric identity is engaged, we tend to become more transactional and *quid pro quo* becomes our primary currency. This identity prompts a one-up or one-down relationship with others and leads to an implicit hierarchy between people. The motivational hub when operating from this identity is the individual self. "What do I feel? How does it affect me? How do I look?" These are the critical questions.

Another salient question is how aware are we about the intersectional and multi-dimensional nature of identity? Multi-dimensionality is a frame to capture the nuances of our complex inner lives while intersectionality captures the external structural identities. Awareness of intersectionality enhances awareness of nuances of our identity and how we define ourselves and others. It also allows us to connect with others because an understanding of our identity as a dynamic and textured phenomenon may afford opportunities to find commonalities with almost anyone or at the very least, help us appreciate the complex identities others hold and be more sensitive and empathetic to that.

G writes a complex phenomenological reflective account of her identity and how the practice helps her clarify and move through dynamically,

> [t]o take a moment to stop and reflect thoughtfully about my experiences and where I've been in order to know where I am trying to go. I did that during the retreat where I was even brought to tears when realizing what a rich and fulfilling life I've had thus far ... All steps to some degree are concepts derived from radical self-love that some of my favorite Black feminists (Audre Lorde and bell hooks) have always written about. "Commitment to truth telling lays the ground-work for the openness and honesty that is the heartbeat of love. When we can see ourselves as we truly are and accept ourselves, we build the necessary foundation for self-love." – bell hooks ("All About Love") ... It never comes easy to talk about my authentic and ideal self in public, especially with a group that may have different life experiences than me or who see the world differently than I do. But what was compelling about this in-person retreat was a realization that in such a polarized world, everyone struggles with vulnerability, hardships, and self-love. I thought a lot about today's cancel culture and even my participation in this form of denouncement. Personally, there are some non-negotiables that I will not tolerate if violated with intent, such as upholding anti-Black, anti-Indigenous, and anti-Immigrant sentiment, and practices which not only happen with white people but as well as in POC communities. Through this retreat, I really started contemplating the need for restorative justice practices in our movement spaces with our BIPOC communities and white accomplices. I think we should be moving away from denouncement and [towards] understanding people's right to humanity. I would like to explore this further in the movement spaces I subscribe to and I think contemplative practices like the ones we engaged in the retreat could be a good start.

Who Is In Our In-Group?

Tribal-centric identity is tied to our affiliations, kinship networks, familial networks and even work organizations. For the select others who are in our in-group, we tend to extend benevolence and suspend transactional expectations. Tribal identities foster strong in-group identities and cultures and lead to social cohesion. Most in-groups do not need an out-group to define themselves but need a boundary that separates the in-group members from others. My friend Alison was a New York Yankees fan. She had season tickets for the Yankee games for decades. She went to their spring training. She followed the team obsessively. Part of Yankee identity is their historic century-old fierce rivalry with the Boston Red Sox that began when the Boston Red Sox owner sold the player Babe Ruth to the New York Yankees in 1919! These affiliations are governed by affect and may be even counter to logic. After their sale of Babe Ruth, a previously successful Red Sox went without a title for close to a century creating the superstition of the Curse of the Bambino. But when we get stuck in the tribal-centric identity system and it becomes our go to or core identity, we tend to unwittingly fall prey to the divisive dynamics of Us Vs Them. We are not advocating to cut ourselves from our tribe but learn how to be anchored and grounded in it while also being expansive, open-minded, and universal.

To do: What Is Your Core Self?

1   How much do you identify with the following? Use a five-point scale (1 — not at all to 5 — very much)

    a   Your immediate family
    b   Your organizational affiliation (work, church, volunteer, sports, etc.)
    c   Your community (local, geographic, ethnic, racial)
    d   Your compatriots — fellow country men and women
    e   All of humanity
    f   All of universe including the planet and all the living things

2   When they are in need, how much do you want to help? Use a five-point scale (1 — not at all to 5 — very much)

    a   Your family
    b   Your organizational affiliation (work, church, volunteer, sports, etc.)
    c   Your community (local, geographic, ethnic, racial)
    d   Your compatriots — fellow country men and women
    e   All of humanity
    f   All of universe including the planet and all the living things.

3   Who do you donate most to? Use a five-point scale (1-not at all to 5 — Most)

    a   What, donate? I work hard to protect my family's financial secur-ity and future.
    b   Your organization — alumni organization, church, etc.
    c   Your community — local food bank, local charities, your ethnic group associations, etc.

    d   National philanthropic organizations – United Way, etc.

    e   International Red Cross and other international relief and rescue organizations, fundraising campaigns for private individuals you do not know.

    f   Animal shelters, Nature Conservancy, etc.

Plot your scores. Which items received the most 1s? which received the most 5s? What did you learn about your core identity? Are you more egocentric, relationship-centric, tribal centric or interdependence-centric?

How do you see the relationship between your Identity (Q1), Intention (Q2), and Action (Q3)? Is this your ideal self?

Notes

1 Kaplan, H. S., Hill, K., Cadeliña, R. V., Hayden, B., Hyndman, D. C., Preston, R. J., Smith, E. A., Stuart, D. E., & Yesner, D. R. (1985). Food sharing among ache foragers: tests of explanatory hypotheses. *Current Anthropology*, 26, 223–246. doi:10.1086/203251.
2 Schutte, N., & Barkhuizen, N. (2015). Knowledge Management and Sharing in Local Government: A Social Identity Theory Perspective. *Electronic Journal of Knowledge Management*, 13(2), 130.
3 Banerjee, D., Saha, S., & Dasgupta, P. (2005). Reciprocal resource sharing in P2P environments. *AAMAS '05: Proceedings of the fourth international joint conference on Autonomous agents and multiagent systems*, 853–859. doi:10.1145/1082473.1082603.
4 Poonamallee, L. C. (2011). Impact of Collective Socio-Ecological Beliefs and Values on Societal Compassion in Disaster Management. *Academy of Management Best Paper Proceedings*, San Antonio, TX.
5 Pattillo, M. E. (1998). Sweet Mothers and Gangbangers: Managing Crime in a Black Middle-Class Neighborhood. *Social Forces*, 76(3), 747–774. doi:10.1093/sf/76.3.747.

Chapter 8

Embodied and Embedded Identity

We live in our bodies and in communities that made us and communities of our making. In this chapter, we look at the embodied and embedded nature of our identities.

Body awareness is inseparable from identity understandings.[1] Experience of the body and its stability in the moment is integral to self-confidence and agency to define oneself and act upon those notions.[2] Our body is a map that cues us to our own selves and the environment. It is key to both self-awareness and relationality.[3] New scientific discoveries about our brain provide more insight into how our brain is built for connection, attunement, and attachment.[4] Even those who are challenged in the areas of emotional self-awareness can be taught to pick up on their emotions through cultivated attention to their bodies.[5] Embodiment is thus a form of tacit knowledge.[6] In a world that weaponizes one's own body, one's identity is of course tied to it. It is especially poignant when we think about our brothers and sisters who are vulnerable to attacks because of their skin color, body shape, hair texture, or gender identity. I grew up with Fair & Lovely advertisements in magazines and on TV in a society that prized whiteness.[7] My parents were always more confident about getting my lighter skinned sister more easily married than me sporting slightly darker skin. Then there were my cousins who were darker than both of us whose parents were advised to save a lot of money for a dowry. When a baby was born, the inevitable first question in my community was, *Kozhandhai nalla color-a irukka?* (Is the baby fair colored?) *Nalla* color also means good color – fair is good; fair is lovely. Even today, Indian matrimonial advertisements casually list skin color as a selection criterion. Agency and body ownership are strongly tied together.[8] In a world that is hyper-connected through technology, we lose touch with the embodied nature of our existence. Body awareness is inseparable from self-awareness.[9] I occasionally feel like a giant head walking around instead of a head attached to a body that feels different sensations including pleasure and pain and even grew another living being inside itself. Our bodies are only homes on the planet, but we are mostly disconnected and distracted from it. We lose the history that our body geography provides because our attention is drawn to other things. Even pain is a reminder that we are beings in our bodies. Sometimes physical pain is an emotional language showing us what we feel, what we like, and what we fear. While understanding that several of us struggle with our bodies and the trauma these struggles leave on our psyche, I have found that participants in my program appreciate this connection and attention to the body. I particularly like the grounding that planting our two feet on Mother Earth provides and how we can draw strength from the universal mother. I would recommend trying a brief body scan to see how it feels if you are new to the practice. It is a great practice whether you are on the run and need to reground yourself or in bed at the end of the day as a great way to destress and thank your body for supporting you during the day.

One participant fell in love the very first time. He kept returning to it over the period of the program.

> I enjoy body scans. Focusing on the pressure where my body touches the floor and couch. It helps me be in the moment and can shrink my world down to the couch ... I know where I carry stress in my body, and when I am stressed I can ignore those parts of my body for some time, which is to my detriment. I dive into my body, paying special attention to my legs and back. After the body scan, I try to do some stretching briefly. I feel good and limber.

Another participant who had a very powerful and transformative experience, writes about their experience.

> For the first two days of practicing the full-body scan, I listened to the 5-minute video in the morning and then Dr. Poonamallee's video at night. Over the week, I started this meditative exercise without the aid of the videos. I went through the order of focusing on each part of the body described in Dr. Poonamallee's video. I could feel the days' tension releasing at night. As the week progressed, I started just doing the body scan in the evening when I would get home from school and/or work. Going into this practice after coming home and settling in allowed for a more meaningful evening routine internally but also externally. I felt like I had more energy to engage in conversation with my partner to debrief our days, I didn't feel angry or annoyed if something didn't go as planned during the day, and I even felt like I could concentrate more doing my homework readings for school. I think the best part was being able to sleep quickly and have a good night's uninterrupted sleep. I think moving forward, I would like to continue this practice.

I find accessing the body very useful to reduce anxiety and facilitate renewal or reconnection to practice and for cultivating emotional self-awareness. I cannot highlight how important it is to include journaling as a supportive sense-making process to scaffold and hold your hands gently through this program. If you are a leader or leadership development professional, treat the participants with compassion and empathy, and acknowledge how precious the journey is. Here is a story of self-discovery about the participant's resistance to body scan:

> I really felt aware of my body during meditation. And it wasn't necessarily a positive experience. In one body scan meditation, I didn't enjoy the awareness I felt in my body, but rather, I felt deeply uncomfortable and irritated when bringing my attention to each body part and sitting there in my skin. Every time I focused on a new body part, I would suddenly feel the urge to scratch or stretch that particular area ... Then, when doing the body scan meditation, I couldn't help but think to myself that my body was angry with me for neglecting it ... which then of course made me irritated that I was negatively judging my experience and not following the "judgement-free" guidelines of meditation. I feel that I often self-sacrifice my own wants and needs in order to avoid conflict with others around me, and neglect what my own body is telling me. I think I've been doing this for so long, that I'm afraid to actually "tune in" to what my body needs because I feel I've fallen so far behind in my relationship to my physical body. I think I'm afraid of the hard work it will take to get back there ... or maybe it won't be as hard as I think. I just don't really know what I'm waiting for.

What are you waiting for? Try the body scan mediation.

Body Scan Guided Meditation

In this meditation, we scan our body. We get connected to our body. Learn to read what our body shows us. Our bodies house us. Our legs carry us. Our heart pumps blood for us. Let us pay attention to our bodies and develop an intimate understanding.
   Get comfortable in your body
   You can sit, stand, or even lie down
   Close your eyes gently
   Let us begin with three deep, delicious breaths
   Inhale ...
   Exhale ...
   Inhale all the goodness
   Exhale all the negativity
   Inhale ...

Exhale ...
Now focus on your left foot area
Let's begin with your left toes
How do they feel?
Feel free to wiggle them if you feel like it
Can you feel the individual toes?
How does it feel?
Feel the sensation
Can you identify your sensations?
Maybe you stubbed your toe and didn't notice at the time and now you can identify that it hurts just a bit
From the toes, shift your attention very gently to the footbed
In your mind's eye, see what it feels like
These feet carry us
Planted, they connect us with Mother Earth
Imagine touching, massaging your left foot
How does it feel?
How does it feel to connect your mind and body?
Say thank you to your left foot and gently shift your attention to the ankle
How does your ankle feel?
The top of your left foot?
Imagine rubbing oil or salt on the top of your foot
How does the sensation feel?
Move your attention to the calf muscle
Maybe you exercised today after a long time or climbed a few stairs
Perhaps you feel the delicious ache that comes from exercising after a long time
Just pay attention to how the left calf muscle feels
Connecting the mind to the body
Seeing, feeling your body through your mind's eye
In all this, you treat your body in your mind with kindness and gentle curiosity
No judgement
Just observation, acknowledgment
Move up from the calf muscle to the knee
You can always move your knee if you feel like it
We are not prisoners of this practice
But it is a good idea to keep it still for a moment and observe it with your mind's eye
How does the knee feel?
Perhaps you are due for knee surgery
Perhaps you are an athlete and your knees bear the brunt of your running

Say thank you to your knee
In your mind's eye, feel the underside of your knee
The tender part
Next move up to the left thigh
What sensations do you feel in your thigh?
Does it burn?
Does it feel soft?
Does it feel firm?
What about your underside of your thigh?
How does it feel in your mind's eye?
We try to keep our attention to the physical sensations in the body
From the left thigh move to the left side of your lower body
Hip, pelvis, and left buttock
How does it feel?
Our pelvises hold up and support the weight of all our internal organs
The engines and carburetors of our body
How does the buttock feel against the floor or the chair?
Say thank you to the pelvis
Move your gentle attention to the left waist and left side of your torso
How does it feel?
Can you pinpoint and describe the sensations?
Do the sensations feel the same on the front and back of your torso on the left side?
Or does the back feel different?
No judgment
Just gentle curiosity about our own bodies
Now move your attention to the left shoulder and neck area
This is where a lot of our stress sits
Do you feel that?
Or do you feel fluid?
Just pay attention with gentle curiosity
As if it is our body but not our body at the same time
How does it feel?
Next, slide your attention to the left arm
Imagine your bicep
Flex it in your mind
How does it feel?
How does the skin feel in the left arm?
Slide down further to the elbow, arm, hand, and fingers
How do they all feel?
What sensations do you feel?
Can you send some energy down and relax your fingers?
Are they curled or loose?
Pay attention

Our hands do so much for us
Say thank you
Move your attention back up the same way it came down to the neck and then head
How does your head feel?
Heavy? Light?
Is your scalp tingling with attention?
Imagine rubbing your scalp with your fingers
What does it feel like?
In your mind's eye, come down to the forehead
How does it feel?
Then pay attention to your face
Are your eyes easily closed?
Or are you forcing them, squeezed tight?
If you find that, relax and let your eyelids flutter
It is okay if light peeks into your eyes
Pay attention to your cheeks and cheekbones and ears
Imagine fingers raining down your face and behind the ears
Can you feel the parts of the body we don't even think about?
Now pay attention to your nose and mouth?
Is your mouth pursed tight?
Relax your face and your jaw if you find they are tight
Inhale and exhale
Now, move from your face to the neck to your right shoulder
Does your right shoulder feel different from the left?
Send your mind's gaze down the right arm
How does your right arm feel?
Right elbow?
Send your kind, curious gaze down the elbow to the forearm and then all the way to your fingers
Then send your mind's eye up the right arm to the shoulder
From the right shoulder, go down to the right side of the torso
Does your back need a massage?
What does the right torso feel like?
Send your gaze down to the ribs, the waist, and the skin
Next, we are going to try to feel our inner organs
Can you feel your heart beating?
Our hearts work so hard so we can live
My heart also works hard at loving too
Say thank you to your internal organs that keep us going
Now move your attention to the right side of the pelvis
Do your right and left pelvis feel aligned?
Can you feel the right buttock?
Moving from the pelvis area, direct your curious attention the right thigh

How does it feel?
What about the right knee?
Move down from the thigh, the knee, backside of the knee, and move your gaze to the right calf muscle and right ankle
Imagine pushing oxygen down to the tip of your right foot
Go all the way down to your right foot, ankle and then your right toes
Say thank you, foot
Now to wrap up, we are going to pay attention our spinal cord
Start your attention at your navel and slide down and around your pelvis to the base of your spine
Imagine a silver cord of power here
Now imagine relaxing your spinal cord vertebra by vertebra with a lot of love
Your spine is your switchboard
It directs your brain's instructions to all the parts of your body
Move up the spine and come to the top of the spine and base of the neck
Relax your neck if it is tight
Now imagine running your hands from the back of your neck to the front of your neck and then to both sides of your face
Like a mother cupping her baby's face
Send loving energy and pay attention to how your face reacts to this attention
Does it soften?
Does it relax?
End with your fingers fluttering over your eyes
And in your mind's eye, see your entire body as a system of inter-connected organs and parts How does it feel at the end of the body scan?
We conclude with three deep breaths
Inhale ...
Exhale ...
Inhale ...
Exhale ...
Inhale ...
Exhale ...
Now open your eyes gently whenever you are ready
Take as much time as you need
If you are using it at bedtime, it is a good time to go to sleep

******

My personal preference is sitting mediation. Sitting gives us permission to step out of the frantic pace of life we have all convinced ourselves to be the meaning and purpose of life. Even when we run for pleasure or dance for fun, we track our speed, heartbeat, and calories. It is a bit difficult to measure how well we sat – of course we can measure our heartbeat or blood pressure afterwards – but the paradox is that if we were to focus so much on the outcome and get all stressed or excited, our blood pressure is unlikely to drop. However, I also find it useful to break the usual association of meditation as a sitting practice and remind ourselves that our bodies move, run, and walk. That we can be mindful in whatever activity we undertake. A reminder that we can bring mindfulness to all our activities and bring body awareness while in motion and in other ways. For example, a drawing meditation in Part 4 guides you to use both dominant and non-dominant hands to draw. We all know what it feels like to hold a pen or pencil with our dominant hand. Drawing with our non-dominant hand can be a jolt to our system since it is an unusual sensation and novelty can cultivate attention. Where does it ache? Which finger do we put pressure on? Are we a wrist easy or wrist hard wielder of the drawing implement? When you try these, please journal meticulously.

Embedded Identity

Our identities are embedded in socio-ecological systems such as family, community, country, place, landscape, religion, ethnic group, race, or people.[10] This sort of identification with a larger whole, i.e. collective identification, supports depersonalization[11] and facilitates a transition of identity from Self or Personal Identity to Social Identity (I to We) – beyond egocentricism. As discussed in prior chapters, identity is at the center of the mental models that shape our engagement with members of our tribe and the world at large. Sometimes our identity is vested in geography and the connection to a place or people who live in that place or come from it. We ask each other playfully, "are you a beach person? Or do you belong to the mountains?" Environmental psychologists have long understood and discussed the relationship between people and places in depth. Place attachment[12] is a particular form of identity[13] because places have meanings. Positive meanings attributed to places keep people healthy. Place-based identity is not simply history, but it is also the emotional and cognitive reactions a place elicits from us. Such calls are wild and deep. They relentlessly demand our heedful attention. Ecological embeddedness[14] requires personal identification with the land and facilitates ecological respect and stewardship of the natural environment. While place attachment is a real phenomenon, paradoxically, our shared human history is one of migration – from continent to continent, country to country, even state to state, rural to urban – colonizing, co-opting, co-mingling, co-operating, and even supplanting different groups of peoples.

For some of us, our primary identity is embedded not in a place but a culture or religion or our country of origin or adoption. To continue with the Dalai Lama example from the previous chapter, his identity is strongly associated with Tibet and Buddhism. Even though he has never lived in Tibet as an adult, he identifies himself as a Tibetan. As a custodian and the leader of Tibetan Buddhism, being of and from Tibet is a salient one. Part of it is religious identity about Tibetan Buddhism. Religion (or lack of) is also a salient social identity for many of us. Acting as cognitive frames, religion shapes our mental models in a top-down manner. Religious teaching shapes the moral identities of many, and religiosity is almost a proxy for moral worth in many places.[15] A confounding factor is the rise of the nones[16] in today's world when more and more of the younger people identify themselves as unaffiliated to any religion and I have addressed implications for organizations in my work. Many leaders are deeply shaped by their religious affiliation. For example, Dr. Martin Luther King Jr. had a pastor's oratory cadence, and the moral righteousness of a man of the cloth to demand equality in the eye of God. Mahatma Gandhi similarly appealed to the Christian spirit of the British. President Nelson Mandela appointed Reverend Desmond Tutu as the Head of the Truth and Reconciliation Commission in South Africa to investigate the allegations of human rights violation during the apartheid era. A contemporary example is when Senator Mitt Romney stood up as the sole republican to vote for the impeachment of President Trump while invoking his covenant with his god. These examples do not mean that religious identity is always a force for good. From the crusades to the Holocaust to the present-day atrocities in the name of religion including the rise of the Hindutva in India to the anti-science, exceptionalism beliefs of the white supremacists in the US, religious identity has also been the source of division among people. However, good or bad, these socially embedded identities are powerful forces for goodness and to equal measure, strife, and violence.

Without getting into the thorny discussion of good and evil aspects of religion, I want to draw your attention to the fact that religion (and the attendant culture) may be a salient embeddedness system for all of us. It is essential then to reflect on how our identification with any religion, or the lack thereof, influences how we perceive those who either do not belong to our religion or do not believe in any religion. Who is our people? Who is not ours? How do we behave with one group vs the other? We need to examine these essential questions when we reflect on our group or social identity. We can and do have several such social identities including religion, place of origin, nationality, alma mater, organizational affiliation, etc. Such embeddedness fosters specific and targeted collective action to protect the rights or heritage of a group and especially helpful for communities at risk to reclaim, nurture, and protect their cultural heritage. If we were to continue with the example of the Dalai Lama, because of the embeddedness of his identity in Tibetan culture and heritage, he has spent his decades in exile protecting the Tibetan language and culture. He persuaded the Indian government not only to host the Tibetans in exile and educate their children, but also advocated for the inclusion of Tibetan culture in their education. Cultivating such collective identity that binds a group of people is a critical leadership function for cohering people around a common purpose or vision and for building and deploying power for collective action. It is the power-through model of leadership in which leaders exert their power through recruiting members into the collective identity.[17]

The notion of collective identity becomes even more important when there is a violation or infringement. For example, I came of age at a time when my mother tongue, Tamil, was a unifying collective identity not just to the inhabitants of my state (and its politicians) but also to the Tamil diaspora across the world. Even though I was raised in a religious family, I relate far less to my religion than I do to my language and ethnicity as a cultural identity. The Tamil genocide in Sri Lanka had a rawness and realness to the Tamils of my generation. It was not simply news about something happening elsewhere. The struggles of the Tamil peoples in Sri Lanka shaped our political rhetoric and fueled the popular culture. Protests against Hindi being compulsorily taught in Tami Nadu began in 1935 and gained momentum in 1965 when talks of Hindi becoming a sole national language emerged. Successful protests – including riots, deaths, and arrests – followed the indefinite two-language policy (Hindi and English) at the center. These agitators and protestors became the face of the Dravidian movement and the regional parties that have stayed in power from 1967 until today. Born in 1970, I imbibed the language-based identity and the love for my language. I identified with the movement even though I was too young to be personally involved in any of the riots or protests. I view it as an anti-majority victory because Hindi is the most commonly spoken language among Indians, and it would have been easy to give up the fight, but the protestors held firm. Given the Covid-19 pandemic, I have had to give up my usual quota of summertime travel to India. Watching a Tamil movie then becomes even more of an evocative experience than usual. The sounds, sights, and emotional tonality makes me terribly nostalgic for my home state of Tamil Nadu. Like every migrant, my heart is split and resides in many places. Reflecting on this makes me think about tribes and how we evolve within our tribes. Finding your tribe is a potent discourse. Seth Godin[18] wrote a best-selling book about finding, creating, and leading your tribe of passion. When we all grew up and lived in the same place, following well-trodden paths, our identity is embedded in our tribe of origin. People went to the same schools together, probably went to work in the same places, ran around and partied with the same crowd, prayed and mourned together, and in this case, your tribe is the context for your whole life. The human need for a tribe is primal and foundational to our evolution and survival. When we don't have a readymade tribe, or wish to go beyond our tribal trajectories, humans still tend to seek and form new tribes. For example, I belong to the academic tribe. I also belong to a tribe of parents who parent like I do – non-violent and child-led life and learning. Part of me belongs to my Indian roots. Like a tree that grows its roots where it is planted, I also have deep roots and emotional ties to the US. I feel at home everywhere or nowhere, depending on my mood. "Can I find my tribe?" is a haunting question in today's hyper-diasporic world. The act of claiming an identity itself is an act of power. However, it is also laden with nuances. For instance, consider the BIPOC – Black, Indigenous, People of Color – identity. Those who claim it consider it to be more inclusive of all people of color thus bringing together the black and the indigenous, the most oppressed groups in the world. However, there are others who find these larger categories erase their nuanced identities. Simply put, social identity is a collective identity and almost always cannot be separated from discussions of power.

Although tribes provide identity, meaning, purpose, and connection, tribal identities also divide. Unquestioning and unreflective allegiance to any group, idea or a role is a slippery slope to tribalism or jingoism or some kind of -ism that separates us from the universe at large creating a bind of Us Vs Them. In our self-examination, we need to reflect on whether such strong identification comes in the way of positively relating to the 'other,' the out-group members. Yes, it is important to find a community in which we thrive. But unless we move beyond our tribal affiliation, we will never be able to self-actualize and become our ascendant and transcendent selves. Evidence of this divisive nature of tribal identity system is littered over human history and geography. How do we mitigate for our evolutionary tendency to fall prey to tribalism? How do we balance the need to be grounded in our identity and the need to transcend the embeddedness? One way to do that is by intentionally embracing a marginality that can provide the freedom to say yes and walk the edge and cross boundaries. Certainly, our embeddedness is a source of strength and object of commitment, but we also need to be flexible enough to embrace difference in today's changing world.

I am unabashedly optimistic about our capacity for growth, change, and benevolence. We created cultures, civilizations, buildings, art, music, literature, politics, and governments among other artifacts because we share the paradoxically rare and ubiquitous trait of imagination. So, yes, follow your passion, find your tribe, love them hard, and thrive. But let us go beyond our tribes and find ways to connect with other tribes. Because we are capable of it. And we need that ability to expand our moral circles. Paradoxically, to do this, we need to embrace our marginality and deal with our fear of being alone. Embrace our history and identity and not be its prisoners. Consider the indigenous activist, Winona LaDuke, who has been consistently and persistently involved in indigenous activism from 1985 when she founded the Indigenous Women's Network to the more recent Dakota Access Pipeline Protests. Although she did not grow up on a reservation or did not even know the Ojibwe language when she first moved into the White Earth community, she has spent most of her adult life in service to her primary identity group but with a crystal clear understanding of the interdependent web of life that we are all part of. She said:

> Mother Earth needs us to keep our covenant. We will do this in courts, we will do this on our radio station, and we will commit to our descendants to work hard to protect this land and water for them. Whether you have feet, wings, fins, or roots, we are all in it together.

To do:

When you did the identity related exercises in the previous chapters (Who are you? What is your core identity?) what emerged as salient group identities for you? Where are you embedded? What affiliation grounds you? Can you draw a Venn diagram?

Notes

1 Brendel, W., & Bennett, C. (2016). Learning to Embody Leadership Through Mindfulness and Somatics Practice. *Advances in Developing Human Resources*, 18(3), 409–425. doi:10.1177/1523422316646068.

2 Palmer, W., & Crawford, J. (2013). *Leadership embodiment: How the way we sit and stand can change the way we think and speak.* San Rafael, CA: CreateSpace.

3 Van der Kolk, B. (2015). *The body keeps the score: Brain, mind, and body in the healing of trauma.* New York, NY: Viking.

4 Siegel, D. (2012). *Pocket guide to interpersonal neurobiology.* New York, NY: W. W. Norton.

5 Feldenkrais, M. (1972). *Awareness through movement.* New York, NY: Harper & Row.

6 Johnson, M. (2007). *The meaning of the body: Aesthetics of human understanding.* Chicago, IL: University of Chicago Press.

7 Poonamallee, L. C. (2012). Corporate Citizenship: Panacea or Problem? The Complicated Case of Hindustan Unilever. *The Journal of Corporate Citizenship*, 44, 8–28.

8 Tsakiris, M., Schütz-Bosbach, S., & Gallagher, S. (2007). On agency and body-ownership: Phenomenological and neurocognitive reflections. *Consciousness and Cognition*, 16(3), 645–660. doi:10.1016/j.concog.2007.05.012.)

9 Mehling, W. E., Wrubel, J., Daubenmier, J. J. *et al.* (2011). Body Awareness: a phenomenological inquiry into the common ground of mind-body therapies. *Philosophy, Ethics and Humanity in Medicine*, 6, Article 6. doi:10.1186/1747-5341-6-6.

10 Whiteman, G., & Cooper, W. H. (2000). Ecological Embeddedness. *Academy of Management Journal*, 43, 1265–1282. doi:10.5465/1556349.

11 Turner, J. C. (1982). Towards a cognitive redefinition of the social group. In H. Tajfel (Ed.), *Social identity and intergroup relations* (pp. 15–40). Cambridge: Cambridge University Press.

12 Buttimer, A. (1980). Home, reach, and the sense of place. *The human experience of space and place*, 3, 166–187.

13 Lewicka, M. (2011). Place attachment: How far have we come in the last 40 years? *Journal of Environmental Psychology*, 31(3), 207–230. doi:10.1016/j.jenvp.2010.10.001.

14 Whiteman, G., & Cooper, W. (2000). Ecological Embeddedness. *The Academy of Management Journal*, 43(6), 1265–1282. Retrieved August 14, 2020, from www.jstor.org/stable/1556349.

15 Edgell, P., Frost, J., & Stewart, E. (2017). From existential to social understandings of risk: Examining gender differences in nonreligion. *Social Currents*, 4(6), 556–574. doi:10.1177/2329496516686619.

16 Poonamallee, L. (forthcoming). Nuns or Nones? Revisiting Spirituality and Religion in the Workplace for the New Generation. In Goosby, J. E. (ed.), *Questions we ask*. New York, NY: IGA Publishing.

17 Turner, J. C. (2005). Explaining the nature of power: A three-process theory. *European Journal of Social Psychology*, 35, 1–22. doi:10.1002/ejsp.244.

18 Godin, S. (2008). *Tribes: We Need You To Lead Us*. New York, NY: Penguin.

Chapter 9

Insider-Outsider Identity

Oh, the eternal paradox of wanting to belong and wanting to be separate, distinct, and unique. Expansive leaders are reflexive about their own identity and affiliations. They may be from a group and recognize that affiliation but also examine their membership with some detachment and how that membership may shape their actions as leaders and followers. People can simultaneously be insiders and outsiders in relation to a thing or group. As an insider-outsider, we can actively engage in something, while we can also objectively view our own process of engagement. This requires a critical reflection practice. Cultivating the insider-outsider identity allows us to simultaneously own our personal experience and yet bring an objective eye to our own actions and mental models. That way we can own affirmative choices and be brave enough to surface the ambivalences we have with an identity. For example, I am deeply rooted in my Indian upbringing but also painfully aware of the stratified nature of the Indian society, both in terms of caste and gender roles. Similarly, I am a naturalized American, an American by choice not just by accident of birth. I am grateful for the opportunities and the American spirit that has welcomed immigrants, and enshrined individual liberty, but I must also deal with the stain of slavery, the extermination of the indigenous, and the ongoing and systemic racial violence that plagues my adopted country and my role in the structures that perpetuate racism. Examining our own affiliations and our thought processes can be daunting if not outright frightening. Expansive leaders make a concerted effort to be mindful of the traps of -isms so they can transcend the divides and build a more collective approach to leadership. Mindfulness as a critical reflection practice allows us to access that which is invisible, taken for granted, or never questioned. We also begin to notice unhelpful frames, interpretations, perceptions, and habits of our minds. At an individual level this capacity is essential for cultivating that moment of detachment and distance that allows us to overcome our lizard brain response to a stimulus that it perceives to be threatening. Our brain is programmed to minimize expenditure of energy by jumping to conclusions, however false and misguided they may be. This means that someone who doesn't look like us triggers our implicit, unconscious biases that raise our resistance. We become tribalistic in moments of anxiety and terror because we don't know how to connect across boundaries. Us Vs Them is so deeply etched into our evolutionary history. We feel before we think and when we don't know how to slow down our reaction, we act on those feelings instead of managing them.

My father once (or many times) told a story about when he was a young teen worker. Due to his family circumstances, my father began to work fulltime in the Postal Department when he was just seventeen to support his large extended family. At the lowest end of the totem pole, he started out as a night sorter; his job was to manually sort the mail all night so other day workers including postmen could deliver the mail during the day. My father used to ride his bicycle to work and back, coming home in the early hours after the graveyard shift when the whole world was quiet. When passing a public bathroom on his route home, he could see the shadow of the old-fashioned flush tank pull installed on the wall but always first mistook it for a noose that someone had used to hang themselves or as the ghost of a human who had died that way. He described how, as a result of that vision, he was always anxious on the ride home. He sweated, his palms stuck on the handlebar, he imagined he could smell the scent of jasmine flowers and hear the sound of dancers' anklets (both were used to signal the arrival of ghosts in the Indian movies of those days) and he would start pedaling faster and faster as he came closer to the bathroom. One night, he decided to stay late at work and then ride home after dawn. On that ride, he stopped at the public bathroom and saw the noose for what it was – a chain pull for the overhead flush tank. His night bicycle rides changed after that. I am my father's daughter. When I lived in Southern California and learned about dangerous, life-threatening rattle snakes, every hose and rope was a rattlesnake in my mind's eye. Our body and mind work together to keep us safe in the world filled what they perceive to be sources of danger. But, as we have discussed in a previous chapter, our brain possesses neuroplasticity, i.e. it can develop new neural connections and pathways at any age. New information and new experiences have a physiological impact on how our brain works. These findings are encouraging for transcending our conditioned responses.

Mindfulness can help in developing an insider-outsider approach to accessing our own minds, thoughts, and being from a distance. Most novice mindfulness practitioners associate meditation with clearing or emptying of the mind. I tend to direct practitioners to begin with observation rather than a furious attempt to clear the mind. For example, when I teach thought-based meditation, the idea is not to suppress the thoughts but to observe them as if they are not ours. We cultivate attention to our thoughts so we can separate from them. So, we are not attached in an egotistic manner to our thoughts. Viewing our own thoughts from a non-judgmental but critically reflexive stance is useful to check our own fundamental assumptions and mental models. Here are three ways to practice critical reflection.

Counterfactual Thinking

Counterfactual thinking – i.e. imagining alternatives to what has already happened and walk that path in our minds – is a helpful tool. It helps in learning from experience, in decision making and deduction, and in processing complex emotions. Thinking about what might have been is a human condition. Who among us have not thought about how we either missed an opportunity or took it and bungled it? A whiff, a touch, a gentle breeze, someone's child, a couple at the coffee shop holding hands, a distant memory, someone's vacation home, pictures of travel in South America, a grant denied, a gift received, a cupcake eaten, a promise broken, a drink taken, love unspoken, an unkind thought spoken, an expense incurred, a trip deferred, bridges burned – all sorts of regrets lurk through the alleys of our brains. Seemingly unique to one but common to many – regrets about relationships, careers, uncoupled loves, and unfulfilled dreams are pedestrian but powerful. Secret regrets that surprise the holder and the listener. The popular movie, Black Panther, is a powerful counterfactual history. What if Africa was never colonized and Africans were never shipped to the Americas as slaves? What would a successful, prosperous, always-free, technologically advanced African country look like? The film brought to life a possible answer to this question and captured the imagination of millions of people, especially of the African diaspora. What if we were to ask this question about our own life stories in relation to our identities? What would we lose? What would we gain? What an interesting experiment it would be to understand ourselves but also expand ourselves?

To do: Counterfactual Thought Experiment – What If?

- Pick one identity salient to you – maybe ethnicity, gender, class, race, sexual orientation or country of origin, a college you went to, your neighborhood, etc.
- Now, ask a counterfactual question. What if you were not that? If you are gay, imagine what kind of person you would be if you were straight; if your primary identity is that of race (say black), imagine being white. How would that change you? If you come from a financially stressful situation, imagine money was never an issue in your life. How would your identity have shifted? How would your life story have shifted?
- Journal your response. What did you learn from this exercise?
- If you can, find a person who you imagined to be and have a conversation with them about this exercise and ask if your conclusions were correct.
- What did you learn from this conversation?

Dialectic Approach

In the dialectic approach to our thoughts, we examine competing thoughts, perspectives, and identities in a systematic manner and identify the tensions we face in articulating our identities and dealing with the consequences. The goal is to bring to the surface and challenge interpretations and values that support the dialectic. When my then fourteen-year-old son was taking his first cultural anthropology class at the local community college, he learned about societal categories such as individualistic and collectivistic orientations. He then proceeded to write an essay about my emigration from the India to the United States as a graduate student as a seeking of individualism. Although I came in search of freedom from what I perceived and knew to be an oppressive social structure, norms, and expectations, especially for women, I never defined or saw it as an example of my individualistic mindset. My son's analysis of the dialectic challenged my own assumption about my identity! That led to a series of aha moments about my need for acceptance from the family and community that I had run away from, to my relationship with romantic love (always has a price), my strong identification with independence (unwillingness to give up my sole motherhood) and so on and so forth. Not a very original story, unfortunately, but very mind-opening for me. Your details may be different, but the pattern is the same – thesis-antithesis-synthesis, Voila!

This dynamic is very much applicable to other levels of analyses as well. For example, let us consider social entrepreneurship. A new form of organization – social ventures promote both social and financial goals by creating earned income streams to meet social goals. However, these ventures are almost never successful at scaling up or run into mission drift when they attempt to scale up. Scaling up requires investments and investors want financial returns. Exposing the dialectic through both rhetoric and praxis has led to the rise of impact investments and impact investors who are even occasionally willing to compromise on the quantum of financial returns in order to meet social impact goals. This has also resulted in the creation of new forms of incorporation such as the Benefit Corporation, B-Corp, and Low Profit LLC's. Greyston Bakery in New York is not only the first benefit corporation in the state but they explicitly call themselves a social justice enterprise promoting inclusion and battling against systemic inequities.

To do: Thought Experiment – Dialectic

- From your set of identities, find two that have no overlaps at all. Identify the conflict between the two. Or you might think of yourself as anti-racist and an activist colleague called you on your privilege.
- Now dig deeper. Where did the two identity systems come from? What fuels each one?
- What is the source of the conflict?
- Is there any way to resolve the conflict?
- If you cannot find a way to resolve it, can you find a way to live with the conflict?

Dialogic Approach

Our self-concept is stable but ever-changing; it is an ongoing process of construction, reconstruction, and integration of one's life experiences into one's identity. It consists of several independent, self-contained, and some-times opposing and conflicting selves. We carry multiple voices, both indi-vidual and collective in this ever-turbulent space in our minds. Construction of our identity is negotiated through a constant internal dia-logue. For example, "Am I being a good person? Or am I being a fool?" When we approach this process with openness, we may find surprising solutions that transcend the conflicts.

To do: Thought Experiment – Dialogic
Go back to your response to the question, "Who am I?" Think about your relationships and the faces you present to each one based on your identity and reflect on the following questions.

- What questions or relationships do you think most about on any given day?
- How frequently do you think about these questions?
- How important are these questions for you?
- How happy or unhappy do you feel about these things?
- How fulfilled or unfulfilled are you about these things?
- To what extent do you feel your identities contribute to your actions and decisions?
- Do you feel connected to a sense of purpose or community through these identities?
- Do these identities make you feel special or different?

Chapter 10

Moral Identity

Moral identity is the degree to which being moral is an important aspect of one's identity.[1] Not all those who can tell right from wrong always do the right things. Moral identity is the link between moral judgment and moral actions. Expansive leaders develop a moral identity. Our mental models shape how we engage with each other and how moral we think we ought to be with others. As we know, mental models are created by both cognitive processes and affective or emotional experiences, i.e. top-down and bottom-up brain mechanisms. Mindfulness is not just of the mind. It is also heartfulness. In fact, the Sanskrit word '*manas*' means both mind and heart. Some people know something to be right or wrong but may still refrain from moral action. For example, most people know it is wrong to bribe or cheat on taxes, but some are more willing to do that than others. People with a strong moral identity, i.e. their moral values, tend to reduce the gap between their moral judgement and moral actions. This is because the gap makes them feel uncomfortable.[2] Moreover, they look at themselves a certain way and want to preserve their own sense of self about who they are and how they ought to behave. The gap between implicit and explicit moral selves plays a part too. Implicit moral self is automatically activated, and explicit moral self is activated through deliberate moral reasoning.[3] Therefore, unless the individual is capable of great emotional self-regulation and slow or Systems 2 thinking, and/or is in a situation which permits the time necessary for deliberate moral reasoning, they tend to rely on more implicit moral self because it is more easily accessible. Therefore, to be consistently moral, it is important to keep the implicit moral self as high as possible. People who operate on high moral identity may have made it more implicit and accessible by acting in a moral way more frequently. For example, people that exercise regularly tend to want to exercise more regularly. Those who cheat on small things tend to cheat on big things too. Moral self is in a way one's ideal self. People with a high moral identity tend to experience a more expansive sense of moral regard,[4] experience strong moral anger, and react more strongly to justice violations.

Moral dilemmas are different from non-moral dilemmas because they are laden with emotions and challenge our fundamental assumptions and mental models. The most intense emotions occur in personal moral dilemmas in which you are the affected party or the primary actor who causes harm to others. In experiments, participants take the most time to solve or respond to personal moral dilemmas. Moral dilemmas involve both cognitive and emotional processes and the emotions intensify the dilemma and slow our thinking. On the other hand, in an impersonal moral dilemma, i.e. you are a third person or observer, your emotional involvement is not as high as it would be in personal moral dilemma situations. To be a good moral person or leader, it is essential to then identify our emotions so as not to identify with them. Pioneering work on the salience of emotional and social intelligence to leadership excellence has provided a pathway to operationalize essential leadership competencies in actionable and developable ways. It is well proven that emotional and social intelligence competency is the secret sauce that separates the exemplary from average performers as leaders and managers. There are well-validated tools and instruments that measure one's emotional and social intelligence using 360-degree feedback. However, competency approaches are based on how to alter one's behaviors and how others perceive them and not focused on inner transformation, i.e. helping people be better humans or more moral. Unless we do the difficult work necessary for inner transformation, leadership competencies development can become nothing more than a blueprint for manipulative leadership behaviors. It is like giving the charming child the key to the nuclear codes. The world doesn't lack charismatic and narcissistic leaders who are divisive, polarizing, petty, and dangerous to the well-being of all. Even as many private sector organizations are struggling to stay morally relevant faced with societal demands for inclusion, justice, equity, and environmental responsibility, leadership development has mostly focused on and is justified by organizational outcomes defined in capitalistic language. To address this, it is not enough to focus on behaviors. Leadership development must focus on shifting underlying mental models towards inclusion and social justice at all levels. We need leaders who are decent, mature, flexible, and open minded enough and willing to change their minds when they learn new facts. Examination of our moral identities is an essential element of expansive leadership. This critical and honest engagement with our identity holds us accountable to our desire and reduce the gap between our ideal and real selves.

I started to think more about the underlying values, beliefs, and mental models that shape people's behaviors. Human history is littered with charismatic individuals who are emotionally and socially intelligent enough to inspire people to follow them. But without a moral sense of social mindfulness and an idea of social power, they were simply egotists or narcissists who treated their followers as instruments to serve their own egoistic personal power needs. We need leaders who are not only capable of *demonstrating* emotional and social intelligent behaviors but also have a more inclusive and interdependent view about themselves and their role as leaders. How do we develop leaders who are not only skilled at emotional and social competencies but are socially minded, i.e. prosocial and inter-dependence-centric instead of egocentric? How can moving from our narrow perch that is almost always held up by insecurity, anxiety, narrow mindedness, and transactional orientation to a broader connection to the universe at large not be transformative? How can such transformation not be frightening? How do I support such transformation? My work is centered on this purpose.

To do: Unpacking your Moral Identity Exercise

1   What does it mean to be a moral person in your book?
2   Think of a situation when you felt either very positive or very negative emotional reactions to your own moral action or inaction.
3   Describe the situation in detail. What happened? What part of your identity got triggered? Were you part of the in-group or the out-group?
4   If you felt very positive, what made you feel positive about it? What was the overlap between your personal and moral goals in this situation? Would you attribute your sense of well-being to that?
5   If you felt very negative, why? Was there a gap between your personal and moral goals in this situation? Do you attribute your negative feelings to this gap?
6   What was your immediate reaction to the situation? What was your deliberate response to this situation? Did you have time to engage in deliberate thinking?
7   What did you learn from this exercise?

My aim in using mindfulness and contemplative practice is to transcend the instrumental and move toward transformative outcomes, specifically feeling a strong sense of connection to other people – regardless of their ethnicity, religion, gender or any such affiliations – and with the universe at large. At its roots, mindfulness practice is not just about being more pro-ductive in the pragmatic realm. It is about connecting with the vast sacred universe and feeling that connection from the tip of our toes to the top of our heads. Feeling that oneness with the universe is the sacred knowledge experienced and embodied in every fiber and ever cell. When one feels the heart swell with the connection and gratitude for the moment.

It is a powerful experience, as some of the participants testify in their journals.

This week's gratitude meditation felt like an overall cleanse of my mind and body. I felt like I visited every emotion that the body has felt in the past few days. Even through such a stressful week, I felt a sense of security, assurance, and wholeness just by listening to the recording for this week. The one thing that I have noticed is that the meditation that involves the control and awareness of multiple senses at once, seems to work the best for me as compared to the other techniques. I feel more grounded and held together even in tough situations. I feel like this guided meditation helps me focus on it even when I am having a bad day. I can play the voice in my mind at multiple times and have my senses involved in it too. I feel like this works the best, as I can acknowledge the presence and existence of these various senses and be grateful to them for the services they provide.

Sometimes, the bells in the church of Serendipity ring loud.

I've mentioned before how much I like this series from Latha, and I have to say I didn't think I could be more enthusiastic until I listened to the session on gratitude. It's a great example of the universe giving you what you need to hear when you need to hear it.

I spend a lot of time naturally in gratitude, despite my stoicism. I'll never forget what it was like to grow up so modestly in income. I could not walk into a Starbuck's because it was so fancy, we did not belong. I still think of that often, though I have become one of their loyalty customers. I seem to carry a bizarre feeling of appreciation with me that I have to keep under wraps, so I do not make others uncomfortable.

When I think of gratitude in general though, the first thing that comes to mind is the safety of my apartment. I am deeply grateful to have my own space that is safe and cozy and just how I set it. Therefore, I was extra touched by the idea that your body is the only home that we ever truly have. And according to my fortunes to date, that home has been overall very strong and healthy for many years. It has gotten me a long way. And no matter where I go, I will have it until the very end, my one and only true home that will have served me so well.

When my mother died in July, my partner's mother also died the same weekend. His mother being Pure Land Buddhist, we began an intensive chanting and praying ceremony earlier that weekend which would go on for days in an effort to provide the safety and peace necessary for his mother's spirit to move on from her body, what would be its former home. There was a lot of focusing on encouraging the spirit to leave its home and not to hang on to it, but there was also a strong sense of gratitude for that home and its service throughout each day of her life. It was a beautiful thing. I'd like to feel that way about mine every day as well. This meditation reconnected me with that feeling.

Mindfulness practice provides the opportunity for feeling a connection to the universe.

This book was born out of the desire to nurture a practice of social mindfulness that advances a more inclusive, just, and equitable world by developing leaders who are expansive in their morality and identity, compassionate and just. One cannot be wise without also being compassionate. Being wise in a socially mindful way is to experience the oneness of all living beings. If we are the oppressor and the oppressed, how can we not be compassionate? If we are dark and light, it behooves expansive leaders to grow the good and for growing the good, one needs to focus on it and feed it deliberately, intentionally, and mindfully.

Expansive leadership is grounded in moral expansiveness in which all of humanity is the in-group. However, identity and human action is more complex than what can be neatly summed up in bullet pointed lists. Peace is not the sole property of Buddhists nor does it mean Buddhism and violence cannot co-exist. The Sri Lankan Tamil genocide blessed by the Sri Lankan Buddhist monks is a case in point. Buddhist monks who orchestrated the non-violent Saffron Revolution of 2007 in Myanmar are also complicit in the genocide and persecution of the Rohingya Muslim community there. Gandhis of the world are flesh and blood human beings just like the rest of us. History has repeatedly and cruelly proved that no leader is perfect. For example, Gandhi, ironically the proponent of non-violence, and religious plurality, and well-known for his influence on great black leaders such as Dr. King and President Mandela, is being outed for his anti-black tendencies and racist writing in his early life. Great leaders are people too. This means that to be expansive, we must be attentive and vigilant about our own worst tendencies and foibles. We also need to be open and benevolent that allows and supports others in their growth. It is not perfection we seek but reflection and progress.

Notes

1 Hardy, S. A., & Carlo, G. (2011). Moral identity. In S. J. Schwartz, K. Luyckx, & V. L. Vignoles (Eds.), *Handbook of identity theory and research* (p. 495–513). New York, NY: Springer Science + Business Media.
2 Stephens, J. M. (2018). Bridging the Divide: The Role of Motivation and Self-Regulation in Explaining the Judgment-Action Gap Related to Academic Dishonesty. *Frontiers in Psychology*, 9, 246. doi10.3389/fpsyg.2018.00246.
3 Ellemers, N., van der Toorn, J., Paunov, Y., & van Leeuwen, T. (2019). The Psychology of Morality: A Review and Analysis of Empirical Studies Published From 1940 Through 2017. *Personality and Social Psychology Review*, 23(4), 332–366. doi:10.1177/1088868318811759.
4 Smith, I. H., Aquino, K., Koleva, S., & Graham, J. (2014). The Moral Ties That Bind ... Even to Out-Groups: The Interactive Effect of Moral Identity and the Binding Moral Foundations. *Psychological Science*, 25(8), 1554–1562. doi:10.1177/0956797614534450.

Part 4

The Journey

Chapter 11

The 28-Day Journey

In this part of the book, you can either take a structured approach as suggested or dip into what you like, what you are drawn to. For a structured journey, I would recommend committing to four weeks and following the prescribed directions for each week. If you are not there yet, you will get there when you are ready. It is completely intentional on your end and the journey is designed with scaffolds to support you. Your journey has two directions. One is inward and the other is outward. We do this simultaneously in these 28 days.

Figure 11.1 Inward and Outward Journey towards Social Mindfulness

Inward journey deepens your personal practice. The goal is to give a taste of different types of meditations for you to try; to provide a structure for daily practice so you can develop your own understanding of how things move for you and what works for you in which context. Be prepared to do daily activities and journaling. This set of exercises will strengthen your mindfulness muscle, and help you develop emotional self-awareness, emotional self-regulation, and critical self-awareness about how you show up in the world. The second direction is to explore your identities and relationships from personal self to relational self to tribal or communal self to universal or expansive self. This set of exercises will clarify your stance, your mental models, your ideal self about how you want to show up in the world, who your tribe is, and how you want to move forward as a leader.

Chapters in this section are organized by weeks for four weeks totaling a 28-day period. Each week focuses on one level of self and social identity system: personal, interpersonal/relational, communal/organizational/tribal, and expansive/universal selves. Each day you have an *assigned meditation, an activity for the day, and a journal prompt.*

I strongly recommend that you begin each day with the meditation and end the day with the journal. Find time for the activity either right after the meditation or during the day but journal after both meditation and the activity are complete. For Days 8 to 14, some of the activities require a buddy or partner. Select, invite, and confirm who will do which activity ahead of time. If you cannot find people to do these activities with, do not fret, just complete the meditation and journaling by yourself. If you are a consultant using this in your training program, you can do it in person in a group context or assign it for virtual partnered work.

I send you my warmest wishes as you embark on this journey. One final reminder: be kind and cultivate a curious mind.

Chapter 12

Personal Self: Egocentricism-Individual (Days 1–7)

Our personal self is foundational to our relationship with ourselves and the world. It is important to become aware of and honor what is non-negotiable, what your boundaries are, what your core identity is so you can become a more expansive leader. During the next seven days, you will explore, examine and occasionally revisit personal identity exercises to develop an integrative understanding of personal self and your mental models influenced by your personal identity. You will learn to distinguish between egocentricism vs personal accountability and examine how you set boundaries when you are anchored in this level of identity. You will engage in several types of meditations, journal every day for the prompts provided, and strengthen your inner resources and repertoire for leadership engagement. I grew up hearing my mother say all the time "How you start is how you end." It makes perfect sense for new beginnings. Give yourself the gift of time for the next 28 days to reflect, to uplift, to soar, and to elevate.

The following table provides a bird's eye view of what you can expect in the next seven days.

Table 12.1 Week 1

Day	Meditation	Activity	Journal Prompt
1	Intention Setting	Who am I?	What did you notice today? What made you happy and hopeful today?
2	Walking Meditation		How was sitting vs walking meditation? What are you drawn more towards?
3	Ideal Self Meditation	Analyze a Leader	What is your highest self? What part of your identity are you most comfortable with?
4	Self-Compassion	Dialectic Identity Exercise	What part of your identity are you least comfortable with? Which do you struggle with? Can you bring some compassion to that part?

Day	Meditation	Activity	Journal Prompt
5	Thoughts-based Meditation	Life Story Exercise	How was your experience with the thoughts-based meditation? Did you find it useful, hard, easy, compared to the others you have experienced so far?
6	Emotions-based Meditation		How was your experience with the emotions-based meditation? Do you find it harder or easier than thoughts?
7	Multi-dimensional Self-Awareness Meditation	Revisit Who am I?	Which spoke speaks to you? How does your individual/personal identity shape your mental model about your perception of scope of impact, time horizon, relationality direction?

Day 1

Intention-Setting Meditation Practice

In this meditation, we are going to focus on flow
   Flow is at that moment when you lose track of time
   When you feel so connected to the inside and outside
   It is letting go
   It is gentleness
   It is supporting
   And today we are going to set an intention to prepare for the hero's journey
   Take a comfortable seat
   Close your eyes
   Straighten your back
   Wiggle your toes
   Take three deep breaths
   Breathe in …
   Breathe out …
   Breathe in …
   Breathe out …
   What is a hero's journey?
   A hero's journey is going from the known to the unknown
   And in this journey, we are going to go from the known to the unknown
   And explore
   In a reflective way
   While also being intentional and deliberate about our practice

Breathe in and breathe out ...
We are now going to try one nostril breathing
Put your finger on your right nostril and gently shut it
Take a deep breath through your left nostril
Switch the finger and let the breath go through the right nostril
Pay attention to your body
How does it feel?
Are your feet planted on the ground?
Are you feeling connected to Mother Earth?
Breathe in ...
Breathe out ...
Because flow is natural
Flow is nature
Flow is when we are so immersed in what we do
Maybe you are drawing
Maybe you are gardening
Maybe you are singing
Maybe you are dancing
And you lose track of time
That moment is effortless but intentional
Breathe in ...
Breathe out ...
And now, imagine flowing like a river
Sometimes gentle, a trickle
But still flowing
Sometimes it is a spring thaw
All the snow is melting
Water finds its own level
It is rushing
Celebrating spring
Breathe in ...
Breathe out ...
Sometimes it is a flood
An eruption
Especially when water is blocked and there is a flood
It is a rebellion
There is just not one way to be water
Water moves
Water flows
Breathe in ...
Breathe out ...
Imagine yourself as a source of energy
You are expanding
Energy is expanding

Breathe in ...
Breathe out ...
You are melting into the moment
Because you lose track of time, place
Because you are so engrossed and connected to whatever you are doing
That is a flow moment
Breathe in ...
Breathe out ...
Think of a time when you felt so much connection
And in sync with the universe
Breathe in ...
Breathe out ...
Let the universe flow through you
As if you are a river
Breathe in ...
Breathe out ...
Let the universe flow through you
As if you are clouds in the sky
Floating, flowing, making shapes and delighting children
Breathe in ...
Breathe out ...
Gliding, moving, shifting directions
Connected
That's what water does
It moves
Breathe in ...
Breathe out ...
Sometimes it has the power to take down every obstacle
Sometimes it has the patience to erode every obstacle
Breathe in ...
Breathe out ...
Feel your connection
Enjoy the movement of being water
Of being clouds
Of the breeze flowing through the woods
Breathe in ...
Breathe out ...
You are the river that is carrying the leaves
Breathe in ...
Breathe out ...
And relax, water has its own path
If you just let it find its own way, it will
Breathe in ...
Breathe out ...

Remember to relax your face
Relax your neck
Relax your jaw
And melt into the moment of connection with the universe
Breathe in ...
Breathe out ...
Connect with your body
Resettle
Are you comfortable?
Are your feet planted on the ground?
Do you feel safe?
Breathe in ...
Breathe out ...
You could be the lizard sunning itself
All there is in the moment
Is the sun and you
You feel the rocks, the warmth and the heat
You feel the sun beating on your back
You lift your face, your lizard face, your crocodile face to the sun
And soak it all in
Your breathing slows down as if you are a cold-blooded animal
Breathe in ...
Breathe out ...
You are the woods
Preparing for winter
Quiet
Shedding leaves
In anticipation
In anticipation of being enveloped by the snow
Quiet footsteps of the curious red fox
Breathe in ...
Breathe out ...
You are the river
You are the clouds
You are the woods
You are the wind
You can be gentle
You can be forceful
You can destroy
You can move through
All effortlessly
Breathe in ...
Breathe out ...
I trust that I am the river

I am in flow
I just need to let it flow
I trust that I just need to let it flow
I have intuition
Because I am connected to the universe
Because I am connected to my deepest desires
My greatest ideas
Breathe in ...
Breathe out ...
I trust I am the river
I am flow
I am in flow
I just need let it flow
I trust I am energy
Energy of the universe channels through me
I remember the time I was in flow
Breathe in ...
Breathe out ...
It could be the time you solved a problem at work
It could be the time that a solution for a work problem came in your dream while you were still sleeping
Breathe in ...
Breathe out ...
I am energy
Energy of the universe is channeling through me
Energy never goes away
It can take different forms
It morphs, it changes directions
But it never goes away
It changes states but it is still energy
Breathe in ...
Breathe out ...
Life is energy in flow
I am life
I am life now
I am life in flow
I trust
I own it
I let go.
I hold it
I let go
Breathe in ...
Breathe out ...
Take three deep breaths

Sit straight
Honor your body
It has served you well
Breathe in ...
Breathe out ...
Breathe in ...
Breathe out ...
Breathe in ...
Breathe out ...
I am life
I am in flow
I trust it
I own it
I let go
Because life is a paradox
By letting go, we own it
Breathe in ...
Breathe out ...
Now think about setting an intention for this journey
When you are going to be working on this project?
Breathe in ...
Breathe out ...
Set an intention for what you want to happen
How you want to join this process
Breathe in ...
Breathe out ...
Set an intention for what your hero's journey is going to be
Set an intention not for the end goal but for the process
Set an intention for how you are going to commit to this process
By being present
By being vulnerable
By being open
By being brave
Breathe in ...
Breathe out ...
With a last juicy delicious breath, open your eyes when you are ready
Breathe in ... Breathe out ...
Thank you for joining this practice.

******

Daily Activity: Who am I?

You may have completed this earlier in Chapter 3, but we revisit this exercise with a better understanding of the fundamentals. It is a key question we revisit not just through the 28 days but beyond. This is also an excellent exercise in dyads and groups.

- Step 1: Who am I? Ask this question of yourself at least nine times to unpack your identity. Every time you answer this question iteratively, write your answer down.
- Step 2: How do these identities overlap?
- Step 3: Rank your identity systems. Alternatively, you can also do this as Venn diagram or concentric circles to identify overlaps, and connections.
- Step 4: Think of your most recent important decision or moment. Reflect on what identity systems played a part in how you handled the situation or conflict.
- Step 5: What did you learn about yourself?

Day 2

Walking Meditation

In this practice, we are going to try walking meditation
We begin this period of walking meditation with simply standing
Being aware of our weight being transferred through the soles of your feet to the ground
Become aware of all the subtle movements
That go in order to keep us balanced and upright
We took a long time to get upright and standing
But very often we take it for granted
The ability to stand upright
But just for us individually, it took a couple of years to do this
Become aware of your effort to maintain the balance
Once you have connected to your body and through your body to the ground
We can begin to walk
Fairly slow and then in normal pace
In a normal manner
We are not going to change how we walk
We are simply going to be aware of it
You have no destination
So it could be a very short path
First of all, keep attending to the soles of your feet

Become aware of the alternating patterns of contact and release
Being aware of your foot making contact as the heel first makes your contact
As your foot rolls forward
And travels through the air
Be aware of all the sensations in your feet
Not just the movement
But the contact between the toes
The sensations inside your shoes
The fabric of your socks
Let your feet be as relaxed as you can
Become aware of your ankles
Notice the quality of sensations in your joints
As your foot is on the ground and as your foot travels through the air
Let your ankle joints be relaxed
Make sure that you are not holding tight in any way
Become aware of your shins, your calves
You can be aware of the contact with the clothing
Become aware of the temperature of the skin
You can become aware of your muscles
Notice what your calf muscles are doing
You might even want to exaggerate what the calf muscles are doing
Just so you can connect with that sensation
Then let your walking go back to normal rhythm
Encourage your calf muscles to relax
Then you become aware of your knees
Noticing the qualities of the sensations in your knee joints
Expand your awareness to your thighs
Being aware of the skin
The contact with the clothes
The temperature
Being aware of the muscles
Notice what the muscles in the front of the thighs and what the back of the things do
Once more you might want to exaggerate the actions of the muscles for a few paces
And then letting your walk go back to your normal rhythm
Become aware of your hips
Relax your hips
Even when you think they are relaxed, relax some more
And notice how this changes your walk
You can become aware of the whole of your pelvis
The movements in your pelvis
One hip moving forward

And then the other
One hip lifting and the other sinking
And you can become aware of the complex, three-dimensional space
your pelvis is carving out as you are walking forwards
The lowest part of your spine is embedded into your sacrum
You can feel the spine extending upwards
The lumbar spine
The thoracic spine
You can notice how it moves with the pelvis
Your spine is in constant motion
It is swaying from side to side
There is a twisting
There is a constant, sinuous, sensuous motion
Notice your belly
You might feel your clothing in contact with your belly
Very often our feelings are down there
While we are up in our heads
Seek to what extent you feel your belly is the center of the body
Notice your breath
Keep taking steps
Notice how your chest expands and contracts
Notice how your shoulders move with the rhythm of your walking
Let your shoulders be relaxed
Let your shoulders transfer your movements down the arms
Let your arms swing naturally by your side
Notice all the motions in your arms
Your upper arms
Your forearms
Your elbows
Your wrist
Your hands
Keep walking
And feel the air coursing over hands and fingers as you swing your arms
Become aware of your neck
And the muscles supporting your skull
Notice the angle of your head
Notice how, when you relax the muscles in the back of your neck, your
chin slightly tucks in and your skull comes to balance
You might want to play with the angle of your head and see how your
experience it
Keep walking
You might notice that when you tuck your chin into your neck, your
experience becomes darker and more emotional, more inward turned and
somber

*If you lift your chin up and hold it that way, you might find that your
experience becomes much lighter*
You might become aware of the outside world
Or much more aware of your own thoughts
Keep walking
Bringing your neck back to balance
Relax your jaw
Relax your eyes
Gently focus your eyes
Looking ahead and not staring at anything
*Not allowing yourself to be caught up with anything that is going past
you*
You can be aware of the feelings you are having
Not the emotions but just tones
Are the feelings pleasant or unpleasant?
Notice sensations in your body
See if they pleasant or unpleasant
Just notice them
Don't cling to them
Don't push them away
Just notice them
If you notice things in the outside world
Either pleasant or unpleasant
Just notice them drift by without following them
Or averting your gaze from them
You can notice your emotional states
Are you bored?
Are you content?
Are you irritated?
Are you happy to be doing what you are doing?
Again, just notice whatever emotions are present
Notice your mind also
Is your mind clear or dull?
Busy or calm?
Are we thinking of things unconnected with this practice?
Or are we centered on what we are doing just now?
No judgement
Just noticing them
In a few seconds, I am going to ask you to come to a halt
A natural halt
Not freezing
You are just allowing yourself to come to a stop
Come to a stop
And experience yourself standing

Notice what it is no longer to be in motion
Notice once more the complex balancing act that is going on to keep you upright
Feeling once again
The weight traveling down the soles of your feet into the earth
Simply standing, experiencing yourself
Finally bringing this meditation session to a close with a deep breath
Inhale ...
Exhale ...

******

Daily Activity: Who Am I?

- Who am I? Ask this question of yourself at least nine times to unpack your identity. Every time you answer this question iteratively, write your answer down.
- How do these identities overlap?
- Can you rank your identity systems? Alternatively, you can also do this as Venn diagram or concentric circles to identify overlaps, and connections.
- Think of your most recent important decision or moment. Reflect on what identity systems played a part in how you handled the situation or conflict.
- What did you learn about yourself?

Reflect: Did your self-definition change? How? Why do you think it changed?

Journal Prompt

How was sitting vs walking meditation? What are you drawn more towards? Why? What does this tell you about your embodied identity?

Day 3

Ideal Self Meditation

In this meditation, you are going to focus on your ideal self
Take a deep breath
And imagine yourself in your favorite spot
It could be the beach, it could be the woods, it could be on the water
Imagine feeling open with curiosity
You know that it was going to be a wonderful day

A special day when you were going to discover something new
Get comfortable, relaxed
And joyously open to possibilities
To what life brings to you
Maybe the stars are shining
And a bonfire is going
You can feel the beautiful cool breeze from the water
The ocean, the lake
Maybe you are on a sailboat
The blue waters, the blue skies
Just the way you like it
Maybe you are fishing
Maybe you are hunting
Feel the flow in your favorite spot on earth
You are comfortable, grounded, safe
Safe enough to be open and curious
You are calm and relaxed
Your body is relaxed
Your mind is alert
There is no stress
There is no anxiety
Just calm curiosity
Look! Who do you see?
Right across the water on a sailboat
Or walking towards you on the beach
The gait looks familiar
The person looks confident, happy, successful, and comfortable in their own skin
They are happy with who they are
The person looks familiar to you
Imagine the person is you, ten years from now
Carrying themselves with confidence, comfort in their own skin
Joyful, playful
In flow with the world
They might have regrets
They have made peace with it
They know that life is a long game
They can make it up
Imagine yourself ten years from now
If that person can give you a clue to your world
What it is going to be like?
If you went for your dreams
If you followed your passions
If you got what you wanted

If there were no boundaries
You could be anything you wanted
What would that person look like?
What would that person tell you?
Ten years from now
That other person knows your future
The adventures you went on
The new things you learned
What your relationships look like
What your professional life looks like
What challenges you had to overcome
What gave you strength to overcome the challenges?
Maybe they got a great job and found a career they loved
Maybe they met the person that they are supposed to spend the rest of their life with
Maybe they climbed Mount Everest
Maybe they were on the first mission to Mars
Maybe they live in a beautiful house by the water you always dreamed of
Whatever your seemingly ridiculous dreams
What if they had achieved them?
What can that person tell you about living your life today?
Because they have the wisdom
Having walked your life, the next ten years
Listen to them
Listen to what they have to tell you
Listen to what your life looks like ten years from now
If you were able to get everything you want
Give them a hug
Thank you, my friend, for showing me my future
All that I could be
All that I want to be
All that is important to be my best self
To be happy
To be joyful
To be curious
To be playful
To be passionate
To be faithful
To your partner, your faith, your community
To be engaged
To be held in a circle of love
By your family
By your friends
To be held in esteem

By your colleagues
By your peers
Savor that moment
Say thank you
Tell them you will see them in ten years
Take a deep breath
And open your eyes gently

******

Daily Activity: Analyzing a Leader

Think of a leader you know – real, fictional, dead or alive.

- Select a specific decision that they made or an action they undertook and identify what drove the decision or action.
- How did the decision or action affect those around them?
- How do you think they related to those who were affected by their action?
- Do you think they served or serve a larger purpose?
- Would you call them a moral person?
- Are they a good leader? Has your definition of leadership changed in any way?

Journal Prompt

Drawing on your ideal self meditation energy, spend some time reflecting on your highest self. What is your highest self? How would you characterize that? How do you live that self daily? What part of your identity are you most comfortable with?

Day 4

Self-Compassion Meditation

In this meditation, we focus on self-acceptance and self-compassion
  Find a comfortable position and notice how you are sitting or standing
  Notice how you are feeling physically and mentally
  Take a deep breath in through your nose
  And out through mouth
  Take another breath
  And allow your breathing to relax you as you exhale fully
  Breathe in gently
  As you breathe out, let the air carry your tension out of the body

Continue to breathe slowly and gently
As you begin to focus on relaxing your body
Notice where your body is tense
Focus your attention there
As you breathe, picture that part of your body as slightly more relaxed than before
With each breath, that part of your body becomes a little more relaxed
Imagine what the relaxation feels like
Soft, gentle, calm, loose, free, and let that relaxation feeling grow
Scan your body for any areas of tension
For each area, let the relaxing breath soften the muscle as they give up their hold
Let the feeling of relaxation grow
Spreading calm throughout your body
Breathe in relaxation
Breathe out tension
Let all the tension go as you exhale
Continue to breathe slowly and gently
Deepening your state of relaxation
More and more
With each breath
Deeper and deeper
More and more relaxed
Calm and at peace
Now, begin to create a picture in your mind
Imagine a place where you feel completely at ease
A place you have been
A place you may have seen
Or completely imaginary
Picture this place where you feel happy and calm
Create the details about this place in your mind
Visualize the sights, smells, and sounds of your place
Imagine how you feel physically
Enjoying being still or relaxing
Or whatever enjoyable activities you engage there
Enjoy the way you feel safe in this place
You feel calm and safe here
At peace with yourself
Remain in your peaceful place
While you meditate and build your self esteem
Imagine all the following affirmations are true for you
Right now, in this moment, enjoy the self-esteem relaxation in your mind
Repeat each affirmation after me with conviction
Use your imagination to fully believe the self-esteem relaxation affirmations

I am at peace with myself
I appreciate who I am
I value myself as a person
All people have value
I am a valuable human being
I deserve to relax
I deserve to be happy
I embrace my happy feelings
I embrace being content
I imagine and believe that all these affirmations are true for me and enjoy the self-affirmation relaxation that I am experiencing
When my mood is low, I accept my emotions and recognize that the low mood will pass, and I will be happy again
I look forward to the good times
My future is bright and positive
I look forward to the future and enjoy the present
I look back fondly at many memories from the past
I forgive myself for my mistakes
All people make mistakes
I used to feel regret for some of my mistakes because I am a good person and I always want to do the best I can
And now, I have learned, and I have moved on
I am still a good person
I have released the feelings of regrets
I forgive myself for errors that I have made
Because I have felt bad long enough for them
I have suffered enough and now it is time to be free
By freeing myself from past mistakes, I can move on and do good things
I forgive myself
I believe that all these affirmations are true in this moment
I feel good about who I am today
I accept my flaws and I accept myself
I view my shortcomings as strengths not yet developed rather than weaknesses
I eagerly develop my strengths
I imagine and believe that all these affirmations are true for me in this moment
I approach challenges with strength and not anxiety
I do my best at that time
I also accept my imperfections in what I do
My efforts are good enough and they are okay
I do not have to be perfect to be a good person
I am a human being with flaws
I enjoy being who I am

I nurture the child within me

I feel secure with who I am and do not need to compare myself with others

All the strengths I have heard are present in me today

I still have the same positive character even if not all my strengths are shown right now

I have all those strengths of character and will use them again

I imagine and believe that all these affirmations are true for me right now

I accept myself

I care for myself

I take time for myself and enjoy it

I deserve time for myself

I feel good about taking this time regularly

I handle difficulties with grace

I allow myself to experience and express emotions, both positive and negative

I accept myself

I am perfect the way I am, and I accept myself

I am a valuable human being

I feel confident

I accept myself

I feel secure

I accept myself

Think again of your peaceful place

Picture yourself enjoying the place accepting the affirmations

Any positive feelings or negative feelings, you can still feel calm and at peace

Now it is time to leave your special place but know that you can return to it at any time when you need to

Take with you the feelings of self-compassion, self-esteem, and continue to feel positive

Hold onto these positive feelings of acceptance as you return to your day

In a moment, I will count to three and increase your alertness and you will become fully awake on the third count

One

Take a deep cleansing breath and exhale ...

Two

Take a deep breath and exhale ...

Three

You are feeling calm, refreshed and confident

******

Daily Activity: Dialectic Identity Exercise

- From your set of identities, find two that have no overlaps at all. Identify the conflict between the two. Or find a situation in which your personal identity got challenged. You might think of yourself as anti-racist, but an activist colleague called you on your privilege.
- Now dig deeper. Where did the two identity systems come from? What fuels each one?
- What is the source of the conflict?
- Is there any way to resolve the conflict?
- If you cannot find a way to resolve it, can you find a way to live with the conflict?

Journal Prompt

What part of your identity are you least comfortable with? Which do you struggle with? Can you bring some compassion to that part?

Day 5

Thoughts Meditation

In this meditation, we focus on our thoughts
   Our brain has the capacity to observe the natural flow of the mind and the contents of our mind. It is called witnessing.
   This process allows us to access a deeper state of mind while building more self-awareness
   It is a simple process
   Close your eyes
   Get comfortable
   Take three deep breaths to ground you and to stop rushing
   Inhale ...
   Exhale ...
   Inhale ...
   Exhale ...
   Now, begin observing your individual thoughts
   Witnessing has three steps
   You observe the individual thought
   You label them
   And you let go so you can dive deep into the still and silent consciousness
   Beyond the mind and its thinking process
   It might seem hard
   But it's not
   The more you can become witness to your thoughts

The less control the thoughts have over you
Increasing your freedom of choice
It also weakens the deep habit patterns that block you from being mindful
As usual, be patient and kind
You can do this as a sitting practice to cultivate the mind
But you can access this at any time you need to
Again, witnessing thoughts does not mean suppression or repression
Just observation
Observe your thought
What is going on?
Label the thoughts
Are they useful?
Or not useful?
When you label a thought not useful, it is not being negative about your own thoughts or about you or your thought process
It is naming the thought pattern for what it is
If it is a positive thought, it is a positive thought
If you have a positive thought, a useful thought, acknowledge it
If you are labeling your thought not useful, then do nothing
Just let it go
No guilt or judgement just let go of a thought that doesn't serve you well
Positive thoughts lead you in the direction of growth
Remind yourself while you continue to practice this
You will find it becomes non-verbal, it becomes easier to differentiate between thoughts
Just say the words internally
Thoughts come
And thoughts go
Your mind is awake when you witness your own thought process
This is a way to train your own mind
To see whether your thought is useful or not useful
This is how you move from your body to conscious mind to unconscious mind
It is about self-observation
Identify and label your individual thought
We cannot really escape our mind
So witness it
Face your thought process
You are not your thoughts
You can observe them
As usual, in all mindful practice
You have to find out for yourself
Try it

And own your truth
What kind of thoughts are in your own mind right now?
Knowing where your mind is now tells you how to get where you're going
Are you disturbed?
If you are disturbed or restless, or troubled or wandering
You could characterize that and label it
I am severely disturbed
I am mildly distracted
Or you could be in a dull state of mind
Or you could be distracted
Your mind is flitting from here to there
When you see your own thoughts and your own mind
You understand
When you are attracted to something
Or you are averse to something
Just bring your mind
Observe, label
Even if you continue to be distracted, it is okay
Just be aware of your own state of mind
What are you thinking right now?
Can you observe your own mind?
And see what you are thinking?
Label it
Can you move from a disturbing or distracted thought to a more light,
illuminated, and positive action-oriented one?
If your mind is overly active or noisy, you want to allow that to pass
To transform to clarity and illumination
If your mind is clear, you want to gently maintain the state of mind
If your mind is heavy, acknowledge it
Label it
You want to move towards lightness
It is not good or bad
It is useful or not useful
Another question you can ask is
"Is this particular thought colored or not colored?"
What is a colored thought?
Colored thoughts have a negative valence
They have a disturbing quality
You might have an emotional attraction to one or other
You might be attracted
Or you might have an aversion
So if the thought is not connected to I or Me, that usually means it is a
colored thought
The not colored thought is a neutral thought

That means you are not attached to it
It is just data
And you are not reactive
Sometimes through practice
Your previously colored thoughts have may have lost some of the coloring
That means you have developed a neutral attitude to that thought
So simply observe the individual thought
That flows in the stream of your mind
Rises and falls
And ask yourself
Literally ask yourself
Is this thought colored or not colored?
The goal is to train your mind by internally labelling it
So a thought arises
You ask, is this thought colored or not colored?
Maybe the answer is "colored"
Then ask yourself, is this thought useful or not useful?
If the answer is not useful, then train your mind
You can tell your mind
"This thought is not useful, you can either let go, explore or cultivate the thought"
This may be a slow process, but it builds up over time
If your current thought is colored and not useful
You can let go of it or you can explore it further
Why is the thought colored?
What valence does it have for me?
If your thought is colored and useful, then you might tell yourself
Yes, this is a good idea, I might pursue this further
If the thought is not colored or mildly colored
Usually the thought itself drifts away
You are intentionally allowing a thought to arise
Let the thought arise
Observe it and then label it
Is it useful?
Not useful?
When you can neutrally witness the entire stream of your thoughts
It is easier to examine individual thought patterns
Then it is easier to go beyond the mind towards the consciousness
The original thought may stay but it might lose its coloring
Its attraction or repulsion
So sometimes the previously troublesome thoughts would become mere memories
Because you can observe them
Then you can ask

Is it a correct thought?
Is it an accurate perception?
Am I seeing the thought clearly?
Is it coming from an uncluttered mind?
Or are there other things in my mind making it hazy?
It could be an inaccurate perception
Incorrect knowledge
Crowded thinking
You can also ask yourself if this thought is a fantasy
An imagery
Sometimes your thoughts come from memories
So observe if your perceptions are clear or crowded
If your mind is fantasizing or drifting to sleep
Or is it just mere streams from our memory?
The store house of impressions we all have
You want to cultivate the capacity to see with clarity
And the first step is to observe your individual thought
So observe your thoughts
One thought at a time
Label it
Is it useful? Or not useful?
Is it colored? Or not colored?
Is it clear? Or hazy?
Should I act on this? Or should I let this go?
You want to remind yourself
Stay awake, stay alert
How can I be fully present and see clearly?
You want to cultivate clear thinking
You want to cultivate correct perception
You want to seek a convergence
To get into the space of flow
It is a psychological state
You can bring it with you to everyday life
Your day-to-day thoughts
Understanding the source of your thoughts
Understanding your own reactions
Understanding if you are clear thinking or hazy thinking
As usual be gentle on yourself
You can practice this any time
You can ask yourself this question any time of the day
And observe your thought
Now open your eyes gently

******

Daily Activity: Your Life Story Exercise, Part 1 – Walking Down Memory Lane

Complete Part 1 either on paper or on a computer but make sure to save your work because we will pick it back up tomorrow.

Step 1: Life Chapters

Think of your life as if it were a book. Divide the story into chapters, at least two and at the most, seven. Give each chapter a name and briefly summarize the contents.

Step 2: Critical Events

Think about the key events in your life, and describe what you were feeling or thinking, who was involved, and what this event says about you as a person.

- Peak Experience: Describe a moment when you experienced extremely positive emotions.
- Nadir Experience: Describe a low point in your life story when you felt despair, guilt, or pain.
- Turning Point: Describe an episode where you underwent a major change, especially a moment that was a turning point in your understanding of yourself.
- Earliest Memory: What is your earliest memory?
- Important Childhood Scene: Describe a childhood memory that stands out for you.
- Important Adolescent Scene: Describe an event from your teenage years that is especially significant or important.
- Important Adult Scene: Describe an event from your adulthood (over 18) that stands out.
- Life Challenge: Looking back over the various scenes and describe the single greatest challenge you have faced in your life. How has it changed you?
- Characters: Describe the people who had the greatest positive and the greatest negative influences on your life story. Think of them as heroes and villains of your book.

Journal Prompt

How was your experience with the thoughts-based meditation? Did you find it useful, hard, or easy compared to the others you have experienced so far?

Day 6

Emotions Meditation

In this meditation, we are going to focus on our emotions

We are always sitting on emotions
They are our foreground and our background
But we hardly ever pay attention to them
Self-awareness is knowing our emotional state and being able to identify it
That is what we are going to do today
Sit comfortably
Close your eyes
Take three deep breaths
In and out
Pay special attention to your abdomen and lungs
You can even touch them
Place one hand on your abdomen and one hand on your chest
Feel them expand
In and out
One more time
In and out
Now, pay attention to what you are feeling
What is your emotional state right now?
Take a little time
Guessing is okay
A lot of times we don't know what we are feeling exactly
But to know that we are feeling some kind of emotion is actually good
It is a good starting point
A lot of times we don't know
So pay attention to your emotion
You can feel a lot of emotions
Painful or pleasant
Delight or joy or happiness or gratitude or love or hopefulness or optimism or empathy
It could also be negative
You could be frustrated with this whole thing
You could be irritated with this practice and feel a certain resistance
Or you could be anxious about it
Or about something that is coming up
Or you could even be feeling aversion sometimes
That happens
And that is okay
But you are just going to sit and acknowledge that emotion
You identify that emotion
The most important thing is that you identify the emotion, not identify with it
That means you don't act out on it
The emotion doesn't become you
You, your brain, your mind, your thought process can see the emotion

That is identify *and not* identify *with your emotion*
It is something that is passing through you even if it is longer term
When you can identify your emotion
The next thing you can do is to identify your emotion's location in your body
A lot of times, our bodies give us the clues
Even when we are not aware of our own emotions, our body gives us the clues and sometimes it outright screams
If you are anxious and pretending not to be, you might feel a gripping, tightening, or burning sensation
For lot of people, stress goes to their shoulders or neck or stomach
For many, anxiety goes to the stomach as well
Butterflies in the stomach
Good excitement, anticipation
Sometimes it is too much
It is churning because we are nervous
We are making the body, mind, emotion connection
Pay attention
Where are we feeling it?
Sometimes we feel kind of nervous and we want to giggle
To release the tension
Or you have energy, you want to rock or move because you are not comfortable with the stillness
The discomfort with stillness could just be boredom
Why am I sitting to observe the emotion?
I have no emotion, I am just bored
So observe the boredom
A lot of the time emotions manifest as bodily pain or symptoms, psychosomatic
Your body is as much engaged in the emotions as your mind is
So, identify your emotions
Just observe them
Even knowing that you are feeling something is okay
So what are you feeling?
Where is it sitting in your body?
Maybe right now you are getting impatient or irritated with this meditation
That is okay
Just pay attention to the impatience and irritation
You don't even have to ask why
We all have a range of emotional life
Sometimes it is disgust
Sometimes it is adoration
Just identify it

Stay with it
Feel the feeling
Sheer awareness puts you outside of your comfort zone
Just acknowledging it puts you out of your comfort zone
Can you step out of your comfort zone?
Can you be open to that?
Be with the emotion
Show a mirror
Shine a light
Can you be present to your own emotions?
A gentle gaze on your emotion
Not judgment
Whatever you are feeling is valid because you're feeling it
Positive or negative
Anything you are feeling is legitimate
You don't have to legitimize it
You don't have to explain it
A gentle gaze
A gentle curiosity
A gentle compassion to yourself
The cause of the emotion is irrelevant
You don't have to ask "why am I feeling this way?"
That is not important in this context
Just feel the feelings
Feel it in your body
Develop self-awareness about your emotions
Let go of the idea about the emotions
The why is irrelevant
It is the what
Can you actually identify it?
Do you know what you are feeling?
Can you stay with it?
Can you go to the place of deep stillness?
Where you can be comfortable with yourself
And watch yourself
What is going on?
Bring your focus gently to your emotions
You have the tools to do it
You know how to do breathing meditation
You know how to do body scan
You are finding another layer
You are combining body scan
Looking for where your emotion sits
Where does it show up in your body?

You feel it you will know before you feel it
Because your body tells you
Your body is deeply tied to your brain
Your experiences, your memories, and your emotions
So, you are establishing a connection between your emotions and your body
How do they go together?
Your body becomes an instrument for you to understand
It is another clue to your emotional landscape map
It tells you where your stress sits
You feel happy or sad or stressed or frustrated or bored
How does your body act?
Just staying with the emotions
That is a gift
Even if you are irritable, that is okay
Just paying attention
Paying attention to your emotions and its connections to your physical body
You don't have to deal with more than you have to
The key is to be strong, patient, and consistent
Sometimes this practice can open up memories and emotions
You just feel them with no conditions, no judgment
Just unconditional acceptance of your own feelings
No judgment
If you feel jealous, you feel jealous
If you are angry, you are angry
If you are happy, you are happy
You don't have to ask why
You don't have to explain it
You just have to identify it
And be with it
To identify it right now, you must be present in the moment
You can't describe a past feeling
You can't describe a future feeling
You only describe a memory when you are describing the past
Be with it right now
Take a couple of deep breaths
In and out
In and out
Open your eyes very gently

******

Daily Activity: Life Story, Part 2 – Looking Ahead

Pick up the material that you worked on in the Life Story Part 1 and continue work on it using the following guidelines.

The Future

- Positive Future: First, describe a positive future – what would you most like to happen in the rest of your life story? Be as realistic as possible.
- Negative Future: Now, describe something could happen but that you hope does not happen.

Life Theme

Looking back over your entire life story, can you see a central theme or message or idea? What is it?

Journal Prompt

How was your experience with the emotions-based meditation? Did you find it harder or easier than thoughts?

Day 7

Multi-dimensional Self-Awareness

In this meditation, we are going to focus on our multi-dimensions self-awareness. We integrate breath, body, thoughts, and emotions to develop a multi-dimensional self-awareness that we access through our practice. As we get comfortable with this practice, we can summon it at any time by being present.

Get comfortable. Close your eyes and take three deep breaths in a focused way.

Breathe in ...
Breathe out ...
Breathe in ...
Breathe out ...
Breathe in ...
Breathe out ...
As you breathe in and out
Let's look at your five senses in your mind's eye
Think of a moment from yesterday that stands out for you
Examine that moment

What were you seeing? Maybe a bird or butterfly that flew by, or a biker buzzing past in a blur?

Your friend's face and the new mask they were wearing

What did you see then? What are you seeing now? Are you noticing details that you missed yesterday?

I used to take the subway home from work at Union Station. Pre Covid-19, Union Square was always buzzing.

Buzzing with people who are in a rush

Buzzing with people who are just hanging out

Playing chess

Skateboarding

Listening to the Hare Krishna group singing

Someone waiting for a friend, pacing

Talking to a therapist on the phone

On a nice day, people bring their lunches out to the park for a moment of respite in the busy city

There is a lot I miss

What were you hearing?

Perhaps you hear the windchimes in your neighbor's porch

Perhaps breeze rustling through the bushes

Or a pressure cooker whistle; that is a morning musical instrument in India

I have heard snippets of conversations in the Union Square

A woman complaining about her husband to her therapist on the phone "He never listens"

A young person professing the purity of their ideology to their friend

We must decolonize ...

What were you smelling?

Basil in your garden?

Or your wet dog?

For me Union Square always smells of New York

Pizza, chicken and rice, and pee

What were you touching?

What were the sensations on your face and fingers and toes?

Are you noticing now some things you missed yesterday?

Breathe in ...

Breathe out ...

Breathe in ...

Breathe out ...

Breathe in ...

Breathe out ...

Breath is our steadying friend!

Next, let us pay attention to our body

Take a few moments to move your attention to the entire body

The muscles, the bones, the organs, head, limbs and torso
Breathe in ...
Breathe out ...
Think of your breath as a probe that you send out
Begin with your left foot and trace your attention to the top of your head
Move your attention from the top of your head to the tip of your right toes
Breathe in ...
Breathe out ...
Now, let us focus on our emotions
In that moment yesterday
How did you feel?
Angry? Sad? Happy? Jealous? Disgusted?
How did your emotions flow through you?
Do you feel the same intensity now?
How did you change?
Observe your emotions now
Does one emotion persist?
Or is it a parade of them?
How do they fade in and out?
Next, we will pay attention to your thoughts
What were you thinking then?
Do you remember?
What are you thinking now?
What is going on?
Hopes? Memories? Dreams? Images? Longings? Attitudes?
Or are they replaced immediately? What happens between thoughts?
Breathe in ...
breathe out ...
Breathe in ...
Breathe out ...
Now we will pay attention to the people in the story
What is your relationship to them?
How do you feel towards them?
Warm? Cold? Indifferent?
We will extend this sense of connection to the world beyond the story
People
Relationships
Immediate relationships
Family, friends, co-workers
Widen to include your community, your city, country, and continent
Breathe in and breathe out
What is your relationship with the all these groups of people?
Like your breath, body, thoughts and emotions, who you are includes
how you relate to everyone and everything

We close with three more breaths.
Breathe in ...
Breathe out ...
Breathe in ...
Breathe out ...
Breathe in ...
Breathe out ...
Gently open your eyes when you are ready

******

Daily Activity: Revisiting Who Am I?

- Step 1: Who am I? Ask this question of yourself at least nine times to unpack your identity. Every time you answer this question iteratively, write your answer down. How do these identities overlap?
- Step 2: Can you rank your identity systems? Alternatively, you can also do this as Venn diagram or concentric circles to identify overlaps, and connections.
- Step 3: Compare with results from previous iterations. Has your self-identification changed in any way? How? What did you learn about yourself?

Journal Prompt

Which of the dimensions do you find most accessible? How does your individual/personal identity shape your mental model about your perception of scope of impact, time horizon, relationality direction?

Chapter 13

Interpersonal-Relational Self (Days 8–14)

In this chapter, for the next seven days, you will explore your inter-personal-relational self and work with a friend or a partner, or anyone with whom you can explore the activities. These activities can be completed in person or virtually. I would recommend that you select, invite, and confirm buddy/partner participation in advance. The same person does not have to be the buddy for all the interpersonal activities. If not, you can skip the to-do activities and complete the meditation and journals for that week and move forward. Here is an overview of what to expect this week.

Table 13.1 Week 2

Day	Meditation	Activity	Journal Prompt
8	Reflective Communication	Call and Response Storytelling Exercise (with a partner)	Think about a recent time you communicated in a way to build emotional resonance? It could be with anyone. Describe the event in all its details. What made it work?
9	Reciprocity Give & Take		Reflection on call & response storytelling exercise
10	Sympathetic Joy	Mirroring (with a partner)	Sympathetic Joy Journaling prompt
11	Drawing	Best Self Exercise	Check-in
12	Gratitude	Contemplative Art Exercise	Gratitude Journal
13	Rock to Balloon		What makes you anxious about how you treat others or how others treat you?
14	Loving Kindness	Revisit Counterfactual Thinking	How do you act as a follower? What can you do to become a better follower? What are your mental models as a follower? What mental models will help you be more supportive at followership?

Day 8

Reflective Communication

In this meditation, we are going to engage in a reflection communication mediation

This is an interpersonal meditation practice where we focus on a person

This could be done with another person who is sitting with you or you bring that person into your mind's eye

Let's begin with three brave breaths

Interpersonal intimacy can be frightening, and we need to be brave

Inhale ...

Exhale ...

Inhale ...

Exhale ...

Inhale ...

Exhale ...

Bring this person to your mind's eye or look at your partner's eyes

And imprint their face in your mind's eye

Close your eyes

Take three deliciously deep breaths

Breathe in ...

Breathe out ...

Breathe in ...

Breathe out ...

Now imagine the sea of your mind

All the waves churning at the top

The wind is blowing

Birds are cawing

Imagine the sea of your mind

Imagine that below the surface lies your deep and calm awareness

When you go deep down in that place

Imagine you can observe all the activities that come to the surface

Take some time to imagine that

Breathe in ...

Breathe out ...

Your breath is your friend

It never leaves you

It keeps you alive

Breathe in ...

Breathe out ...

It nourishes you

Breathe in ...

Breathe out ...

Now, think of a time when you felt extraordinarily alive
Emotionally alive
It could be a positive or negative emotion
It is maybe something that you struggle with routinely
It niggles at you
Or it could be an epiphany or aha moment
Wow
Maybe it is a story that delighted you
Restored your faith in humanity
A poem that moved you
Or a movie that made you feel so human
Or it was a playful moment
You remember laughter and joy
A time when you were separated from all the anxiety and worry in life
And reveled in the joy of the moment
Maybe you were hanging out with your friend
Maybe it was your dog that made you giggle
Mine does, all the time
Or you heard a child laughing so hard that you couldn't hear her anymore
Or you accomplished something so wonderful that made you so proud
Or you conquered a fear
Maybe a memory that torments or delights you
Maybe you did or said something that you are not so proud of
Perhaps it is an embarrassing memory
Perhaps you feel guilty about it
Perhaps you wish you had done something differently
Perhaps it is an irrational fear that you cannot shake
It could be anything in the range of emotions
From fear to disgust to happiness, joy, and optimism and a sense of faith
Maybe it happened in your church
Maybe it happened in your family kitchen
Maybe it happened when you were fishing outside
Breathe in …
Breathe out …
Now that you have identified that moment when you felt extraordinarily emotionally alive
A time that pops out for you when you ask yourself that question
Imagine a wheel now
Look at the wheel
Maybe you see it in all colors of the rainbow
And your awareness sis the glowing hub
Imagine the wheel being held by your awareness
Every spoke is your attention

That you use to examine
Using the first spoke, examine your sensory knowledge
Bring to mind the time that you have identified, the story
What did it feel like?
Can you remember what happened?
What sensations? Tastes?
Salt in the ocean air
Perhaps it is a taste of the forbidden drink
Do you remember anything about taste?
Now we will move to the smell
Smell triggers nostalgia
What do you remember?
Scent of pine in the quiet of woods
Perhaps it is your grandfather's whisky smell
Or your favorite food that your mom used to make when you were a child
Do you remember the sounds around you?
The music that was playing then
Maybe a bird you heard
Maybe an ambulance you heard
Recall the incident with all its sensory experiences
What did you see?
What did you smell?
What did you hear?
What did you taste?
Now we move to the second spoke to examine the second section of your rim
We are going to look at our body awareness
Try to remember how it felt inside your body
Were you trembling with excitement?
Did you feel flushed or warm?
What did it feel like inside when you made the perfect turn on the snowboard?
Or the first jump into the river?
Or the first person you asked out?
What did it feel inside for the first loss you experienced?
How did the body feel?
Was your stomach jumpy?
Did your throat feel constricted?
Maybe tears in your eyes that you tried to control?
Do you remember how your lungs felt?
Your heart, your organs?
What did it feel like to inhabit your body at that time?
Can you bring that to mind?

Now we move to the next layer
Your inner mental awareness
What were you thinking at that time?
What was going on?
What were you feeling?
What were your emotions?
What other memories does this incident bring up for you?
Draw on your emotions and thoughts meditation
Can you label the emotions?
Can you label the thoughts?
Can you identify if the emotions were useful?
Did they have color? Did they have valence?
Do you feel strongly about it?
Did it bring up any memories as you were going through the incident?
Now we on move to the relationship awareness
Use the last spoke and examine how you were connected to yourself and others
Does your story have people in it?
What role did they play?
How did you feel towards them?
What was your relationship?
What is your own relationship to the story?
Ask yourself
How do I feel connected to myself and the people in that story in that time?
Now, bring to your mind your own face from that moment
Think of your other self from the story looking back at you
As if you were in a mirror
Instead of looking at it, what if the reflection is looking at you
Do you feel separate from the person?
Separate from the incident?
It may be a strange thing to imagine
But the great thing about our brains is that you can imagine anything you want to
Now, slowly let your other face go from the mirror
Instead bring your reflective partner's face in the mirror
Imagine them looking back at you
Imagine you looking at them
Imagine you looking at their story as if you are watching a movie
What do you think happened in their story?
What does it feel like to be looked at by someone else so intently, so deeply?
Do you feel nervous?
Do you feel angry, joyful, sad?

Observe that person in your mind's eye
How would it feel if you were telling your partner your story and they were completely open to you?
And they grant you their full and complete attention and empathy
Promise your partner, your fellow human being, the same attention and empathy
Pay attention to their face and mind
Promise them you will be non-judgmental about their memories, stories and secrets
Promise them your complete attention. We are all human, after all
Now gently open your eyes and look at your partner

******

Daily Activity: Call and Response Storytelling With a Partner

This is an adapted version of the West Indian storytelling tradition[1] that engages the audience in the storytelling process. We apply this technique in the context of interpersonal mindfulness, engaged communication, and building brave and fun intimacy.

Pick a person with whom you feel comfortable and safe enough to be open and transparent. Invite them to play with you for two days in this call and response storytelling exercise. We are going to do this in digital format. A smartphone or computer is enough to participate in the digital story-telling exercise.

- Step 1: You will record a short audio/video story lasting not more than five minutes that you think you want to share with your partner. You can draw on your life story exercise, but it can also be something that happened yesterday at work or at the store or what your dog or cat did. In short, the tone and content of the story is yours to choose. You will share this story with your friend.
- Step 2: Partner listens to/watches the digital story.
- Step 3: Partner records a response story for you to listen to or watch. They can tell any kind of story. The only condition is that it must be for you and in response to your story. Same rule, not more than five minutes, a short and sweet video or audio. And they share with you.

You can stop with this for the day and pick it up tomorrow. Or you can keep continuing iteratively cycling through several call and response stories.

Journal Prompt

Think about a recent time you communicated in a way to build emotional resonance? It could be with anyone. Describe the event in all its details. What made it work? Did you think about your partner in today's activity more frequently than usual? How did it make you feel towards them?

Day 9

Reciprocity Meditation

In this meditation, we are going to focus on giving and receiving – reciprocity
 Give and take is the root of relationships
 It is done to develop our compassion, our kindness, and open up our being to kindness
 Take a comfortable position
 Close your eyes
 And focus on your breathing
 Breathe in …
 Breathe out …
 When you give and receive, you begin to be open, and accept others and yourself in a more kind, and understanding way
 Open your mind to receiving help
 People are willing to invest in you
 Asking for help is the biggest advocacy action you can do for yourself
 Think of the people and the loving and supportive relationships in your life
 Those who are willing to support your growth
 Be a cheerleader
 A facilitator
 Mentors and sounding boards
 As you inhale
 Accept the help
 During exhalation
 Send your well wishes to those who are giving you the help
 Send your gratitude to those who are willing to help
 You can do both
 Deeply and lightly
 Inhale …
 Exhale …
 Imagine that you are breathing through every cell of your body
 And your cells have permeable boundaries
 Inhale the warmth, compassion, support, love, affection, and the regard from those closest to you

Those who support you
Those who want the best for you
And as you breathe out
You give the same affection, love, support, and consideration to them
Reciprocity
To give and take
Receiving requires humility
Understanding that you cannot do everything by yourself
That you need help
Asking for help is standing up for yourself
But also practicing humility
A lot of us are trained to be strong, independent
With steel in our spine
I invite you to melt that steel
Be a river that flows
Be light that refracts rather than an unmoving, immobile spine of steel
Humility and mercy
Humility and compassion
Humility to receive
To ask for help and to receive it
Bring to your mind the person who is on the top of your list
Feel the connection with them
They may be your child, your parent, your friend, your grandmother
Your teacher
Your spouse, your partner
Be one with them
Send them love
May you be safe
May you be healthy
May you never be separated from great happiness
And receive their love
Their affection
Their regard for you
When you receive their love
You melt that steel
You don't need that steel
People that love you and support are part of your being
Send a deep, cool, spacious, healing breath to your friend
Let the outbreath pour through every pore of your body
Breathe out spaciousness, openness, kindness, and surrender
Breathe in love and affection that comes from people closest to you
Breathe in ...
And breathe out ...
Say thank you

To those who have helped you
To those who you know will help you
As the hardness dissolves, your heart gets more alive
With humility you get support
Imagine this person sitting right across from you
Both of you have your eyes closed
And you are connecting through your hearts
Breathe in ...
Breathe out ...
Imagine your breath is synchronized with theirs
You are connected
Your heartbeats regulate each other's
Be a breathing presence for all beings
As you sit across from your friend
Breathe in ...
Breathe out ...
Notice your feelings, your fears, your ego
But remember the depth of your commitment to them and their commitment to your well-being
Breathe in ...
Breathe out ...
Stay in the moment
When you are ready
Let your mind's eye rise to meet the eye of the friend sitting across from you
Be present
Gaze into the eyes of your friend
Let your good heart connect with their good heart
There is shared humanity in suffering and greatness
Connect with that humanity in that person who is present for you
Be with this person
Close your eyes
And focus on your breath
Imagine this person as a child
They probably had the same dreams you had
They probably needed the same kind of help you needed
Breathe in ...
Breathe out ...
They are your friend, your parent, your child, your partner
Breathe in ...
Breathe out ...
Your heart of compassion is wide open
Your heart of humility is wide open
To receive help and to give help

Give and take
Breathe in love
Breathe out kindness
Breathe in love
Breathe out kindness
Now, open the focus of your practice to the universe
Breathe in universal suffering and compassion
Dissolving your own self-importance and ego
Give away all your goodness to all beings
Giving and receiving is one of the richest and bravest practices that we can do
Giving requires mercy and compassion
Receiving requires humility and self-compassion
Breathe in ...
Breathe out ...
Cultivate these relationships
Not instrumentally
But by genuine compassion
By giving you will receive
By asking you will give them the gift, the joy of them giving you something
In a reciprocal relationship, the gift of giving and receiving, both are there
Sometimes they need something from you
But it is okay
You can pay it forward
You can receive
There are no rules
Except humility and compassion
Breathe in ...
Breathe out ...
The people in your list
They are your cheerleaders
Your witnesses
As you pursue your life, your vision, your goals and dreams
Bow your head to your heart
For such relationships are of the heart
Breathe in ...
Breathe out ...
Thank them for holding you in their circle
A circle of affection, warmth, friendship, fellowship
Giving you kindness and compassion
In the next exhalation, you send your love, friendship, kindness, and compassion

Giving and receiving
Reciprocity
Breathe in ...
Breathe out ...
Take your time to open your eyes slowly
Breathe in ...
Breathe out ...

******

Daily Activity: Call and Response Continued

- Step 4: You listen to/view the story that your partner made especially for you.
- Step 5: In response to the story, you create a loving, personalized story video or audio for them. As always, the rule is that the story must be in response to what they shared with you. A brief, five-minute story. Record and share.
- Step 6: Your partner listens to or views the story, composes a response and sends it to you.
- Step 7: Schedule a time to chat in person or by video. Begin by thanking your partner for participating in this activity with you. Share how it felt to keep them in your mind all day. Ask them to share their experience. Conclude by discussing both your responses and learning from this exercise.

Journal Prompt

What did you learn about yourself and your activity partner in the Call & Response storytelling exercise? Do you feel that cultivating attention towards a person increases warmth or affection towards them as well? Or not? How did this exercise feel? Did you have fun?

Day 10

Sympathetic Joy Meditation 1

In this meditation, we are going to try cultivating sympathetic joy
Sympathetic joy is being happy at somebody else's happiness
Feeling joy at someone else's good fortune
It is one of the most difficult concepts and practices
Because we are so conditioned to compare ourselves with others
So conditioned to treat the world as a competitive space
So someone's good fortune, someone's accomplishments

Something that makes someone else happy
Feels like it is diminishing us somehow
It is also because we are so used to feeling inadequate
Feeling less than
Because when the world is organized by hierarchy
Someone is better than the other
Someone is on top of another
And because we see this as a divided world
Because we don't see ourselves as one with the universe
We see ourselves as divided and separate
If that is the way the world is perceived, it is difficult to feel joy at someone else's happiness
Because they are not us
We are not happy
It is their happiness
This is kind of conditioned
Sympathetic is the opposite of jealousy and envy
Envy and jealousy come from comparisons, division, inadequacy
Seeing, even momentarily, everyone as separate versus one makes it hard to be happy at someone else's happiness
But we are one
By Mother Earth
Whose big breath gives us all breath, life
The prince and the pauper
The oppressed and the oppressor
The saint and the scoundrel
We are all part of the same tapestry
When we share in someone else's joy, we feel part of their happiness
And for that one moment at least, we are not separate from them
We are going to try and feel that
And take joy at other people's joy
As usual, we start with the breath
Take a comfortable position
Close your eyes
Take three deep, delicious, and generous breaths that connect us to the universe and Mother Earth's breath
Breathe in ...
Breathe out ...
Breathe in ...
Breathe out ...
Breathe in ...
Breathe out ...
For good measure, because sympathetic joy is a bit difficult to feel for many of us, let's take one more deep breath

Breathe in ...
Breathe out ...
Now think of a time when you were happy
So happy
It could be something very small
It could be something very big
The trigger itself doesn't matter
It is the happiness you felt
Bring to mind your beautiful face when you are happy
What does your face look like?
How does it feel in your face?
Do you feel warm?
Do you feel flushed in your face?
How does it feel?
Experience that moment
Bring to your mind a moment of happiness
How does it feel in your face?
In your body?
In your heart?
Now, think of someone that you know feels happiness at your joy, your success
Think of someone who is most happy with your good news
That friend, that parent, that teacher, a mentor, or partner
Who feels joy at your joy?
Bring to your mind their face
How do they react to your happiness in the moment?
What does their face look like when they are so happy for you?
Does their face beam with happiness for you?
Does their face radiate generosity of spirit?
Imprint that on your mind
How do you feel when someone is happy for you?
And it shows
How does it make you feel?
Grateful? More happy?
Say thank you for sharing in your joy
Thank you for doubling your happiness because you reflect it back
Say thank you to the universe for giving this person to you in that moment
Someone that cheers you, supports you, someone that can show sympathetic joy to you
Now recall a moment when you saw them happy
Which made you happy
Recall how their face shines when they receive your sympathetic joy
When they feel one with you because your happiness mirrors theirs

As we know our brain has mirror neurons that multiply every emotion
Radiant joy at others' happiness
Pay attention to this person's joy because you are happy for them
That is being one in joy
Say thank you to them for giving you an opportunity to share in their joy
Say thank you for giving you a joyful moment
Breathe in …
Breathe out …
Breathe in …
Breathe out …
Breathe in …
Breathe out …
Breathe in …
Breathe out …

******

Daily Activity: Mirroring With a Partner

Get someone to participate with you in person or via videoconference. Ask them to provide 20–30 minutes of their time to participate. Share these instructions with them.

- Step 1: Look into each other's eyes for a moment.
- Step 2: You are the leader in the first round. Your partner is the follower.
- Start moving your hands, legs, body – move as the spirit does. Your partner will follow or mirror your actions.

Set a timer for two minutes.
Go.

- Step 3: Now switch roles. Your partner is the leader. They start moving their body and you follow.

Set a timer for two minutes.
Go.

- Step 4: Now go back to being the leader. Include emotional expressions in your face. If you are doing the exercise via videoconferencing facility, just do the emotional expression.

Set a timer for three minutes. You lead with emotions and they follow.
Go.

- Step 5: Reverse roles. They are the leader and you follow.

Set a timer for three minutes.
Go.

- Step 6: Discuss how it felt to be the leader and the follower. Did you feel more responsibility or agency or empowerment as a leader vs a follower? Did you feel any kind of connection or attunement? Does your experience support the science?

Journal Prompt (adapted from Dr. Mahaligham's exercise)

Think of a person whose happiness you care deeply about. Write a brief paragraph about that person, your relationship with them, and why you care about them and rejoice in their joy. Describe what it means to feel that joy. What would it take to feel that for others in your life? Set an intention to cultivate sympathetic joy.

Day 11

Drawing Meditation

In this meditation, I am going to guide you through an arts-based meditation
  It is drawing meditation
  You don't need to be an expert at drawing
  You don't have to be interested in drawing
  This is just another form we are going to try
  We will begin with body awareness and then move to drawing
  Before you close your eyes
  Pick up a piece of paper, and a pen or pencil
  And put them on a desk or table in front of you
  Now close your eyes
  Firmly place your feet on the ground
  Focus on your body awareness
  Start with three deep breaths
  In and out
  In and out
  In and out
  Now start with your left toes
  And then spread your awareness to your left foot
  Left ankle, the calf, the shin, the knee, and the thigh
  Switch your awareness to the right foot
  The right toes, the whole of your right foot

The ankle, the calf, the shin, your knee, and your thigh
Center your attention on your pelvis
See how you are sitting
Are you slouched?
Do you feel any pain?
Sit up straight but comfortably
Then send your awareness upwards
See how your stomach feels
Your lungs, your chest
Your lower back
Direct your attention to the middle and upper back and the shoulders
If you feel any pain, relax it
Bring your shoulders down and not keeping them scrunched up helps you relax
And relax your neck and your head
Relax your jaw and face
Now pay attention to your dominant hand
It is right for some and left for others
Starting at the shoulder, move all the way down to your fingers
Then pay attention to your non-dominant hands
Start at the shoulders and go down all the way
Now pay more attention to your shoulders, your neck, your jaw
Relax everything
Direct your attention to the fingers in your dominant hand
How do they feel?
Now without opening your eyes, pick up the pen or pencil with your dominant hand
How does it feel against your hand?
Hold it as if you are going to draw on the paper in front of you
And see how it feels
Do you like writing with your hand?
Do you like drawing with your hand?
Now take three deep breaths
Inhale …
Exhale …
Inhale …
Exhale …
Inhale …
Exhale …
Now start scribbling on the paper in front of you with your dominant hand
Pay attention to what it feels like
Forget about if it is going to be good or not
Forget about it you are doing it right or not
Just let your hand move and draw

Whether it is straight lines or curves or figures or anything
Just let your hand guide you
You just pay attention to your hand
How it moves
And now don't forget to focus on your breath
Imagine your breath is moving through your body to the dominant hand
the fingers that hold the pencil
Continue drawing
Do a quick scan of your body
How do you react to a creative challenge? Creative practice?
Are you tense?
There is no need to be
You are not going to share this with anyone
This is between you and your paper
You don't need to worry about how everyone else does on this
If you are tense, relax again
Use your breath and body scan to relax
When you are satisfied
Turn the paper over
Switch your pen or pencil to your non-dominant hand
The one that we don't use very often
Now use your non-dominant hand to draw
Same thing
Deep breaths
Relax
Let your non-dominant hand flow
Pay attention
How does this hand and fingers feel?
How does the wrist feel?
Does it feel different from your dominant hand?
Does it feel comfortable? Uncomfortable? Strange?
Just label that
Continue drawing with your non-dominant hand
Send your breath down to the fingers of the non-dominant hand
Continue to draw
You might have the urge to peek
You don't have to
Just let your hand draw
You focus on how your hand moves
The hand that is connected to the pen or the pencil
It is an extension of you
How does it feel?
Just continue to draw
Let it flow

When you are satisfied, put the pen down
And do another body scan
Start with the tips of your fingers, hand by hand
The fingers, the palms, the forearms, the elbows, the shoulders
Do the same thing to the other hand
Fingers to shoulders
Just a gentle gaze
How does it feel?
Starting at the top of your head
Go down your face, your neck, your shoulders, your back
Your hips, your thighs
Go down all the way to your toes
When you are satisfied, gently open your eyes

******

Daily Activity: Best Self Exercise

Do this exercise after you complete the ideal self meditation. In this exercise, you will draw on earlier work done on your life story exercise and your interpersonal exercises from this week. Using the images that came to you during your ideal self meditation, develop a composite image of your best self in relationship contexts.

- Who are you in relationships? What is your best self in the context of relationships? What is your highest and most useful purpose in relationships?
- Do you play a specific role in most relationships? Are you more of a giver or a taker, for example? Are you the natural leader in most settings? Or are you comfortable letting others take the lead and going with the flow?
- How do you think others think of you?
- What do you think people around you think are your best characteristics?
- When was the last time someone said something lovely and complimentary about you?
- Does your own perception of your best self mesh with those around you?
- Deliberately and mindfully construct a description of your best self in relationships.

Journal Prompt

You are almost at the halfway mark in this program. How is it working for you? What is easy? What are you finding to be challenging? Who would you like to talk to about this?

Day 12

Gratitude Meditation

In this practice, we focus on gratitude. It is always a good time to practice gratitude. There is no better time than now to practice gratitude. Sometimes, in the busyness of life, we forget to be thankful.
  Close your eyes. Take three deep breaths.
  In and out
  In and out
  In and out
  I want you to bring your awareness to things in your life for which you are thankful
  When you identify the first thing you are thankful for, just let it sink in
  Let yourself sink into the feeling and surrender
  Notice how it feels in your body
  First, be grateful for your breath
  Bring your awareness to the breath
  As you inhale and as you exhale and the fact that your breath is life
  Breath is life
  It keeps you alive
  Then become aware of your heart
  It is strong
  It is resilient
  It beats all the time
  It is beating, it is pulsing, filling with love, filling with blood
  And peace and flowing it all back out
  Bring your awareness to your eyes
  That let you see colors, smiles, nature, the sunrise, the sunset
  The rainbow, the moon, and the stars, and yourself in the mirror
  Bring your awareness to your ears
  That let you hear the sound
  Music, laughter, the voice of loved ones, the silence, and the beautiful sounds of life
  Then focus on your nose
  The smells the ocean breeze brings, the sweet perfume of the flowers, of newly cut grass
  The smells wafting from the kitchen

Now focus on your lips, and your mouth, and your tongue
That tastes, savors, and nourishes
Kisses and speaks, and whispers and sings
Next, bring your awareness to your hands
That hold and touch and hug
That open and close and squeeze
The arms and shoulders that hug and carry and lift and stretch
Our feet, our toes, the gift to wiggle them
Transporting you, walk, run, dangle, dance, kick, leap, and point
Be thankful for your body
It is the only house you have in this world
What about your emotions?
Your joy
Your sorrow
The strength that helps you make it through every day
Say thank you to your emotions
That guide you
That shape you
Then bring your awareness to your abundance, your expansion, your evolution
Your perspective shifts
The affluence, and flow, and empathy, love and light
And your ability to see growth and potential in every moment
We live in the best time in human history
You are everything you need
Be grateful
Say thank you to your life, your body, and your emotions.
Now, breathe
Feel more grace and ease
Experience the warmth, love and compassion that being thankful brings to your heart
Next, drift your awareness to nurturing relationships in your life
New ones
Older ones
Old friends, family, new friends, your teachers
Your coaches, your partners, your teammates
Say thank you to all the good people in your life
And even those who seem bad at times but give you an opportunity to learn and grow
And stretch your love, your compassion, your empathy
Breathe in ...
And breathe out ...
Send thanks for the material things that come to you unexpectedly
Or things you worked hard for

With great effort, commitment, and hard work
Say thank you to the things that give you comfort, convenience, ease of life
And joy
Think of all the love you have in your life
Your connection to those who are sweet, loving, and honorable and feel
right
That connect you to deep inside yourself, as well as outside of you
When we no longer take life for granted, we become grateful for every-
thing that we have
Just breathe and feel the flow of gratitude
It is always a season for thankfulness
We are blessed with a lot of things
Even if at the moment we feel anxious about the transitions, about the
future
Even if we feel guilt or shame about the past
We are still standing
We are breathing
We are surrounded by people who love and whom we love
We are surrounded by beauty
We are surrounded by abundance
And we are standing
We are breathing
Let the gratitude, thankfulness for your life, for your body, for your
heart, your things, your people, your ideas, your accomplishments, your
success, your opportunities for growth and learning flow through you
Be thankful for all of them and let the gratitude fill your body. your heart
See how it feels
Take deep breaths and when you are satisfied, gently open your eyes

******

Daily Activity: Contemplative Picture Exercise With a Partner – Part I

This exercise works best when you have a smartphone with which you can take a picture and send immediately. You can also take pictures or create art and share at the end of the day if you prefer it that way.

- Step 1: Find a partner who is willing to hold you in their minds and hearts for the next two days. Promise that you will do the same for them. Share this exercise with them. Make a 20-minute appointment with them at the end of Day 13.
- Step 2: During the day, pay keen attention to your surroundings, things big and small that capture your attention, and when you see something

that you think your partner would appreciate or something that you want to share with them, take a picture, and text or email it to them.
- Step 3: Ask them to do the same.
- Step 4: At the end of the day create a collage or album of all the pictures in a sequence that makes sense to you and share the album or collage with your partner.

Journal Prompt (adapted from Marsh[2])

Identify three things (including people) that made you feel grateful today. One condition is that your object of gratitude must be specific, and not broad. Being grateful for a snippet of your favorite music you happened to catch as you were walking to work is acceptable. Gratitude to the band not so much! Being grateful to the hug your teen unexpectedly gave you is acceptable. Not parenthood, broadly. Savor the surprise. Identify unexpected and surprising events.

For each item, reflect upon what makes this one special? Go for depth over breadth. Go for details. Go personal.

If you had read the journal prompt in advance, would you have been more alert to opportunities for gratitude?

Day 13

Rock to Balloon Stress Reduction Reframing

In this meditation, I want to focus on reducing anxiety and stress. We live in a stressful world. We lead stressful lives. There are times of the year when life is more stressful than others. It may be exam time for students, the end of the month for salespeople, fundraising time for non-profits and start-up founders. Things we need to decide. Things that concern us about what happens next.

I want you to take a comfortable position, close your eyes
Take a centering breath
One that anchors you to the earth where you stand, where you sit, one that anchors you in your body, one that anchors you in your life
Now take three deep breaths
Inhale ...
Exhale ...
Inhale ...
Exhale ...
Inhale ...
Exhale ...
Now bring to your mind
That which makes you anxious

That which stresses you
That which triggers you
And make friends with that anxiety
That trigger
That stress
If that which stresses you, that anxiety, is your friend, what would your
outlook be?
Or is it already your friend?
That is telling you to protect yourself
That is warning you to be safe
That is protecting you
Is that anxiety or stress dark colored?
Is it pulling you down?
Can you visualize it?
In a favorite color
If it is your friend, what would that color look like?
Imagine if it is a beautiful pink balloon
Your anxiety, your stress
Imagine you are in your favorite green spot or on a beach
The sky is blue
I love the fall light
It may be a different light that speaks to you
I can never tire of fall light
It is potent
It is poignant
It is blinding
It is a gift before winter comes
For some people, fall triggers anxieties
Because they are worried about winter
But whatever light you like
Whatever season you like
Whatever landscape you like
Imagine that
It is a vast, expansive, beautiful, calming, peaceful, gorgeous landscape
The beach
A meadow surrounded by beautiful bright orange maple trees
Now imagine that balloon, that anxiety
That was weighing you down like a rock on your chest
Constricting you, not letting you breathe
Controlling your response
Controlling your sense of agency
Not letting you be self-empowered and powerful
Becomes a friend
A beautiful light balloon

It is pink
It is green
It is silver
It is purple
It is whatever your favorite color is
Imagine transforming that rock on your chest
That constricts
That holds you down
That is dark
That is heavy
Imagine you have the power and you claim the power
Convert the rock into a balloon
Light, easy, buoyant
Now that balloon is your friend
You are a little kid that played with the balloon
Now you are going to let that balloon go
In that fall light
Spring light
Summer light
Whatever is your favorite
Or it is the dusk and the night sky
Beautiful blanket of stars
You are camping on your dock by the water
Or it is a winter's sky at night
Whatever is your favorite at this moment
Take a deep breath
Let the balloon go
Say, thank you for letting me reframe you
Thank you for being willing to change
From the rock, heavy and dark
To a balloon, light and pretty
I am letting you go
I am connected to thousands of years of ancestors, people, the human race
The evolution
I am connected to Mother Earth
Everything around me, this planet, this ground, these trees
They have stood for a long time
That is what I am connected to
That is what I am rooted in
I am like this tree
I am the planet earth
That has survived, thrived, that has provided the home
That nourishes, gives life

I am Mother Earth
I am a child of Mother Earth
I am like the sky
Beautiful
Sustaining all of us
Protecting all of us
Delighting all of us
I am connected
I am connected to the universe
The anxiety, a trigger
It is fleeting
I believe and I own the power to determine the quality of my experience
I believe and I own the power to make the mountain into a molehill
A rock into a balloon and to let it go
I thank my body
I thank my heart
I thank my powerful mind that helps me be agentic
Self-empowered, fearless
I thank those who came before me
I feel connected to those who came after me
I feel connected to Mother Earth
I feel connected to the trees around me
The flowers around me
The bees around me
The birds around me
I am part of a larger whole
While what seems like a big rock
The anxiety and the stress
It was so big in my head
I am going to make it small
I am going to make it light
I am going to let it go
Take one more cleansing, revitalizing breath
Inhale ...
Exhale ...
Open your eyes when you feel ready
And have gorgeous day

******

Daily Activity: Contemplative Picture Exercise With a Partner – Part 2

- Step 5: Look at the collage/album that you put together and imagine the exchange as a conversation through pictures. Set an intention to carry that connection and tone with you during the day.
- Step 6: Like yesterday, continue to pay keen attention to your surroundings, things big and small that capture your attention, and when you see something that you think your partner would appreciate or something that you want to share with them, take a picture, and text or email to them.
- Step 7: Ask your friend/partner to the do the same.
- Step 8: Together, view the pictures, and come up with a title for this story or movie as you see. What did you convey? What did you learn about yourself? What did you learn about the other person? What was most enjoyable about this exercise? What was most uncomfortable about this exercise?

Journal Prompt

What makes you anxious about how you treat others or how others treat you?

Day 14

Loving Kindness Meditation

Settle into the awareness of the body and the breath
   Breathe in ...
   Breathe out ...
   Breathe in ...
   Breathe out ...
   After you have connected with the breath
   Feel your body
   Noticing what is there
   Connect your breath to body
   Breathe in ...
   Breathe out ...
   Be open to whatever you can experience in the moment in the body
   Feel the breath moving through your heart
   We first begin with loving kindness towards ourselves
   Allowing our heart to open with tenderness
   Remember your basic goodness
   Maybe you want to remember a time when you were kind or generous
   And your natural desire to be happy and not to suffer
   If you are finding it difficult to acknowledge your own goodness

Look at yourself through the eyes of someone who loves you
What does that person love about you?
Or you may recall the unconditional love that you felt from your pet
And some of us find it hard
If you find it even harder
Use your imagination and picture yourself as a young child
Feel the tender feelings that you would feel towards this young child
As you experience this love
Notice how you feel in your body
Maybe you feel warm or some heat or a smile
Or a sense of expansiveness
This is loving kindness
A natural feeling that is accessible to all of us
Rest for a few moments with this feeling
Of open and unconditional love for yourself
Bask in that loving kindness towards yourself
Breathe in ...
Breathe out ...
What does it feel like to feel the acceptance?
Now, wish for yourself
May I be happy
May I be peaceful
May I be held in loving kindness
May I feel filled with loving kindness
May I feel centered and calm
May I feel connected and calm
May I know the natural joy of being alive
May I be safe
May I be peaceful and at ease
If there are feelings of warmth or friendliness or love in your body or mind
Connect to them
Allow them to grow
Direct the loving kindness to yourself
Then bring to mind a friend or someone in your life who has deeply cared for you
And send your loving kindness to them
May you be happy
May you be well
May you be safe and peaceful
May you be the recipient of loving kindness
May you be filled with loving kindness
Sink into the intention and the heartfelt feeling you have for this person
They have done so much for you
You feel love for them

Affection, warmth, acceptance
Feel the feelings and send them your good intentions
Connect the feelings to the phrases
As you continue, open the circle to someone that is neutral
You may see them regularly but not know them well
They could be a neighbor
Someone at the store
Somebody that you know of, but you don't know
Bring this person to your mind now
And use the same phrases
May you be happy
May you be well
May you be safe
May you be peaceful and at ease
May you receive loving kindness
May you be filled with loving kindness
Sometimes during this meditation you might even feel the opposite feelings
Anger, grief, or sadness
That is a good sign that your heart is softening
Accept that with whatever patience and kindness you can muster for the same feelings
Instead, direct loving kindness towards them
Now bring to mind someone with whom you have had a difficult relationship
Perhaps it is someone you find difficult to like or feel compassion
This is the time to remind yourself that this person is a whole being
They also need loving kindness
As someone who may feel pain and anxiety
As someone who may suffer
As someone as human as you are
See if it is possible to extend the words of loving kindness to these people or this person
May you be safe
May you be happy
May you feel my love now
May you feel loving kindness
May you be filled with loving kindness
Now allow your awareness to spread in all directions
Imagine that you are standing in a vast space
That you can connect to everyone and everything
Yourself, people whom you love
People to whom you feel neutral
People to whom you feel negative
All human beings, all animals

The rich tapestry of the universe
With all the prospects for joy and sorrow
War and peace
Hunger, abundance
Love, joy, anger, everything that composes your mind and the world
And now, send the loving kindness to everyone and everything
May you be safe
May you be happy
May you feel loving kindness
May you be filled with loving kindness
May all beings be filled with loving kindness
May all beings be happy
May all beings be awakened and free
May all beings be safe
Now, come back to yourself
And see how you feel
If you feel the love and the warmth in your body
In your heart, in your face
Sometimes it is even in the toes
Bask in the energy of loving kindness that you have generated
And the people that practice this all over the world have generated
Connect back to your breath
Breathe in …
Breathe out …
Breathe in …
Breathe out …
Enjoy the feeling
Breathe in …
Breathe out …
Take this moment to connect with yourself and with the universe
With love and kindness and compassion
And gently open your eyes

******

Daily Activity: Interpersonal Counterfactual Thinking – What If?

- Pick a relationship that is very important to you.
- Now, ask a counterfactual question: what if you had never met that person? How would that change you? How would your identity have shifted? How would your life story have shifted?
- What did you learn from this exercise?

Journal Prompt

How do you act as a follower? What can you do to become a better follower? What are your mental models as a follower? What mental models will help you be more supportive at followership?

Notes

1   Alcalá, J. C., Austin, M., Granroth, M., & Hewitt, B. (2016). Online inclusive pedagogy: A call-and-response dialogue on digital storytelling. *Education for Information*, 32(1), 71-85. doi:10.3233/EFI-150963.
2   https://greatergood.berkeley.edu/article/item/tips_for_keeping_a_gratitude_journal.

Chapter 14

Tribal or Communal Self (Days 15–21)

During the next seven days, you will explore their tribal or communal self and social identity systems and unpack your mental models in this realm.

Table 14.1 Week 3

Day	Meditation	To-do	Journal Prompt
15	Breathing	Naming Who We Bring	Journal your response to the meditation and the exercise
16	Body Scan	Land Acknowledgment	What is your sense of place? What is your happy place? Exploring relationship with physical environment
17	Thoughts	Revisit What is your core identity?	Journal your response to the meditation and the exercise
18	Emotions		Journal your response to the meditation and the exercise
19	Gratitude		Gratitude journal
20	Ideal Self in Community	Embedded-Self Exercise	How do you manage your boundaries between your individual, inter-personal and tribal identities?
21	Loving Kindness	Revisit Counterfactual Thinking – What if this is not your community?	Reflect on your relationship with the different nexus of embeddedness. How can you become less tribal and more expansive? What would you gain? What would you lose?

Day 15

Breathing Meditation 2

In this meditation, we will explore our breath
  Sit comfortably
  Keep your spine in its natural form
  You don't need to stress about it
  Be very comfortable
  You are in a calm place
  You can sit on the floor
  Or on the chair
  Now close your eyes
  We are going to focus on the breath
  We are already breathing
  We all do
  We are doing something natural
  Nothing forced
  No specific way to breathe
  Just breathe in ...
  Breathe out ...
  Focus on your breath
  Just breathe in ...
  Breathe out ...
  Your mind might wander
  That is okay
  Be non-judgmental
  It is okay if your mind wanders
  Just bring it back to your breath
  Perhaps you hear a voice outside your room
  Your mind wonders
  Who is talking?
  What are they talking about?
  It is natural
  It is normal
  Nothing to worry about
  Pop that bubble
  Bring your mind back to the breath
  Take all the oxygen in
  Expel all the negativity
  Breathe in ...
  Breathe out ...
  Breath is energy
  Breath is life

It keeps us alive
It meets our most primal need
Be appreciative of your breath
That you are able to breathe
That there is oxygen
Stay in the moment
Let grief go
Grief from the past
Focus on your breath
This moment
Tell yourself I am here right now
Just focus on your breathing
Breathe in ...
Breathe out ...
Shut everything else out
Don't worry about your test tomorrow
Don't worry about your deadlines
Don't worry about plans for dinner
Don't worry about what you will do tomorrow
The worries will wait
This moment
It is a gift
A gift to yourself
Breathe in ...
Breathe out ...
Your mind probably already wandered
That is okay
Just bring it back
Breathe in ...
Breathe out ...
That is why we call it the present
Your mind is running away
Just bring it back
Your breath is your lasso
Breathe in ...
Breathe out ...
Say thank you for the oxygen
Say thank you for this moment
Breathe in ...
Breathe out ...
Anger comes from the past
Let it go for this moment
Breathe in ...
Breathe out ...

Focus on your breath
Breathe in ...
Breathe out ...
It is like a metronome
Within ourselves
A rhythm
Just bring your mind to it
And see the movement
And it is okay if your mind wanders
That that is what it is supposed to do
Our minds are monkeys
Just gently bring it back
Breathe in ...
Breathe out ...
Pay attention to your body
The air that enters your through your nose
Fills your lungs with the air
The oxygen that gets pumped through your blood to your entire body
From your head to toe
From limb to limb
Every cell of your body is getting the oxygen
Breathe in ...
Breathe out ...
No pressure
Breathe in ...
Breathe out ...
Your mind wanders?
It is okay
Do you feel weepy?
It is okay
Breathe in ...
Breathe out ...
If emotions keep bubbling up
That is okay
We are emotional beings
Breathe in ...
Breathe out ...
The only way out is through
That is life
That is breath
We can't keep our breath in forever
We have to let it go
Got to get through the breath
That is life

Breathe in ...
Breathe out ...
Don't give up
But don't strive
Be gentle on yourself
Self-compassion is the first thing
Yes, if your mind wanders
Don't beat yourself up
Just gently bring it back to your breath
Breathe in ...
Breathe out ...
Oxygen in
Carbon dioxide out
Stay in the moment
In the moment
Breathe in ...
Breathe out ...
Just breathe in ...
And breathe out ...
It is very easy
Breathe in ...
Breathe out ...
You don't have to think about anything at this moment
Focus on your breath
And how your bod handles the breath
Just breathe in ...
Breathe out ...
My dog wants to go out
Maybe your dog wants to go out too
It is okay
Open your eyes, let him out
And come back
Just keep breathe in
Sometimes things never go as we planned
My dog wants to go out
I let him out
I come back
I breathe in
I breathe out
We never stop breathing
Maybe you are feeling cold
Maybe you want to adjust your body
You are not used to sitting still
That's okay

Breathe in ...
Breathe out ...
Maybe your phone is beeping
Do you want to turn it down?
Maybe turn on the do not disturb mode?
Breathe in ...
Breathe out ...
Just breathe in ...
Breathe out ...
Oxygen in
Carbon dioxide out
Say thank you for this moment
When you focus on this moment
On your breath
Everything else disappears
Just this moment
It is not hard
It is not easy
It just is
Breathe in ...
Breathe out ...
Your mind is thinking,
Why am I doing this?
What is the point of this?
You don't have to answer those questions
Your mind asks questions
That is its job
These few minutes are your time
Breathe in ...
Breathe out ...
You are already breathing
You are already mentally active
If a thought crosses your mind
Take a look at it
But bring your attention back to your breath
Trust the process
That is all you need to do
Breathe in ...
Breathe out ...
Just breathe in ...
And breathe out ...
The dog's back
I need to open the door again for him
Just breathe in ...

Breathe out ...
Don't give out
The only way out is through
That is life
These fifteen minutes of meditation show you the same thing
Trust the process
No need to strive
It is all about attention
And intent
Intent is in your mind
Whatever you feel is valid
You don't have to defend
You don't have to judge yourself
Breathe in ...
Breathe out ...
Are you feeling sleepy?
That is okay
Breathe in ...
Breathe out ...
Enjoy this moment
Continue breathing practice as long as you want
And then gently open your eyes

******

Daily Activity: Naming Who We Bring

- Imagine you are at the center of a circle surrounded by people who lift you up, people who have taught you important lessons, people who have made your ongoing transformation possible, people who have made your presence here (on the planet, to do this exercise, to buy this book, etc.) possible.
- Make a list of people who have played a role in your ability or desire to be here in our space of learning, discovery, and growth (directly or indirectly).
- Write about why and in which ways they are important to you.
- Say thank you to your inner sanctum tribe.

Journal Prompt

If you are doing the breathing mediation after a while, how did it go? What was your emotional, primal reaction to the exercise? Were you surprised by who showed up in your mind's eye?

Day 16

Body Scan Guided Meditation

In this meditation, we scan our body. We get connected to our body. Learn to read what our body shows us. Our bodies house us. Our legs carry us. Our heart pumps blood for us. Let us pay attention to our bodies and develop an intimate understanding.

Get comfortable in your body
You can sit, stand, or even lie down
Close your eyes gently
Let us begin with three deep, delicious breaths
Inhale ...
Exhale ...
Inhale all the goodness
Exhale all the negativity.
Inhale ...
Exhale ...
Now focus on your left foot area
Let's begin with your left toes
How do they feel?
Feel free to wiggle them if you feel like it
Can you feel the individual toes?
How does it feel?
Feel the sensation
Can you identify your sensations?
Maybe you stubbed your toe and didn't notice at the time and now you can identify that it hurts just a bit
From the toes, shift your attention very gently to the footbed
In your mind's eye, see what it feels like
These feet carry us
Planted, they connect us with Mother Earth
Imagine touching, massaging your left foot
How does it feel?
How does it feel to connect your mind and body?
Say thank you to your left foot and gently shift your attention to the ankle
How does your ankle feel?
The top of your left foot?
Imagine rubbing oil or salt on the top of your foot
How does the sensation feel?
Move your attention to the calf muscle
Maybe you exercised today after a long time or climbed a few stairs
Perhaps you feel the delicious ache that comes from exercising after a long time

Just pay attention to how the left calf muscle feels
Connecting the mind to the body
Seeing, feeling your body through your mind's eye
In all this, you treat your body in your mind with kindness and gentle curiosity
No judgement
Just observation, acknowledgment
Move up from the calf muscle to the knee
You can always move your knee if you feel like it
We are not prisoners of this practice
But it is a good idea to keep it still for a moment and observe it with your mind's eye
How does the knee feel?
Perhaps you are due for knee surgery
Perhaps you are an athlete and your knees bear the brunt of your running
Say thank you to your knee
In your mind's eye, feel the underside of your knee
The tender part
Next move up to the left thigh
What sensations do you feel in your thigh?
Does it burn?
Does it feel soft?
Does it feel firm?
What about your underside of your thigh?
How does it feel in your mind's eye?
We try to keep our attention to the physical sensations in the body
From the left thigh move to the left side of your lower body
Hip, pelvis and left buttock
How does it feel?
Our pelvises hold up and support the weight of all our internal organs
The engines and carburetors of our body
How does the buttock feel against the floor or the chair?
Say thank you to the pelvis
Move your gentle attention to the left waist and left side of your torso
How does it feel?
Can you pinpoint and describe the sensations?
Do the sensations feel the same on the front and back of your torso on the left side?
Or does the back feel different?
No judgment
Just gentle curiosity about our own bodies
Now move your attention to the left shoulder and neck area
This is where a lot of our stress sits

Do you feel that?
Or do you feel fluid?
Just pay attention with gentle curiosity
As if it is our body but not our body at the same time
How does it feel?
Next, slide your attention to the left arm
Imagine your bicep
Flex it in your mind
How does it feel?
How does the skin feel in the left arm?
Slide down further to the elbow, arm, hand, and fingers
How do they all feel?
What sensations do you feel?
Can you send some energy down and relax your fingers?
Are they curled or loose?
Pay attention
Our hands do so much for us
Say thank you
*Move your attention back up the same way it came down to the neck
and then head*
How does your head feel?
Heavy? Light?
Is your scalp tingling with attention?
Imagine rubbing your scalp with your fingers
What does it feel like?
In your mind's eye, come down to the forehead
How does it feel?
Then pay attention to your face
Are your eyes easily closed?
Or are you forcing them, squeezed tight?
If you find that, relax and let your eyelids flutter
It is okay if light peeks into your eyes
Pay attention to your cheeks and cheekbones and ears
Imagine fingers raining down your face and behind the ears
Can you feel the parts of the body we don't even think about?
Now pay attention to your nose and mouth
Is your mouth pursed tight?
Relax your face and your jaw if you find they are tight
Inhale and exhale
Now, move from your face to the neck to your right shoulder
Does your right shoulder feel different from the left?
Send your mind's gaze down the right arm
How does your right arm feel?
Right elbow?

Send your kind, curious gaze down the elbow to the forearm and then all the way to your fingers

Then send your mind's eye up the right arm to the shoulder

From the right shoulder, go down to the right side of the torso

Does your back need a massage?

What does the right torso feel like?

Send your gaze down to the ribs, the waist, and the skin

Next, we are going to try to feel our inner organs

Can you feel your heart beating?

Our hearts work so hard so we can live

My heart also works hard at loving too

Say thank you to your internal organs that keep us going

Now move your attention to the right side of the pelvis

Do your right and left pelvis feel aligned?

Can you feel the right buttock?

Moving from the pelvis area, direct your curious attention the right thigh

How does it feel?

What about the right knee?

Move down from the thigh, the knee, backside of the knee, and move your gaze to the right calf muscle and right ankle

Imagine pushing oxygen down to the tip of your right foot

Go all the way down to your right foot, ankle and then your right toes

Say thank you, foot

Now to wrap up, we are going to pay attention our spinal cord

Start your attention at your navel and slide down and around your pelvis to the base of your spine

Imagine a silver cord of power here

Now imagine relaxing your spinal cord vertebra by vertebra with a lot of love

Your spine is your switchboard

It directs your brain's instructions to all the parts of your body

Move up the spine and come to the top of the spine and base of the neck

Relax your neck if it is tight

Now imagine running your hands from the back of your neck to the front of your neck and then to both sides of your face

Like a mother cupping her baby's face

Send loving energy and pay attention to how your face reacts to this attention

Does it soften?

Does it relax?

End with your fingers fluttering over your eyes

And in your mind's eye, see your entire body as a system of interconnected organs and parts

How does it feel at the end of the body scan?

We conclude with three deep breaths
Inhale ...
Exhale ...
Inhale ...
Exhale ...
Inhale ...
Exhale ...
Now open your eyes gently whenever you are ready
Take as much time as you need
If you are using it at bedtime, it is a good time to go to sleep

******

Daily Activity: Land Acknowledgment

Land acknowledgment[1] is a form of gratitude. Acknowledging our debt to those who came before us and understanding our place within the history of the place. The trees around us, Mother Earth, and the oceans preceded us, give us life, and will continue beyond us. We acknowledge our own position in the tapestry. This is also a very helpful method to introduce to organizations of all kinds and create a broader public awareness of the history of the place the organization or people live and work in.

Reflect on why you are doing this land acknowledgment. Are you doing it because this program demands it? Are you doing it because you feel guilty? Or are you doing it to support indigenous communities and/or acknowledge your own ancestry?

Research and find out answers for the following:

*   Who were the original inhabitants of the land you stand on?
*   What is the history of the land?
*   What is the indigenous place name?
*   What is the language?
*   What is the correct pronunciation of the names of people and places?

Find out the history of your own 'place' and your relationship with your place(s). For example, the original inhabitants and owners of the land my present hometown, New York, stands on belonged to the Lenape people.[2] The purchase of Manhattan (then known as Manhatta) by the Dutch was the beginning of the forced migration of the indigenous original inhabitants out of their homeland. As Smithsonian magazine reports, "in one of the most diverse cities in the United States, there are tellingly few native New Yorkers." I acknowledge that I am an interloper here.

On the other hand, my place of birth, Chennai, in India was originally and continuously occupied by people of my ethnic extraction but was raped and plundered by invaders and colonists from the Mughals to the British over centuries. I acknowledge that my community was wronged but I also voluntarily left a land that was home to generations of my ancestors.

Land acknowledgements need not be grim, or guilt ridden. It is an acknowledgement of original owners, articulation of our gratitude, finding our own relationship with a physical location, honoring the truth, and making a commitment to always be mindful of this relationship.

Journal Prompt

What is your sense of place? What is your happy place? Where do you feel your best self?

Day 17

Thoughts Meditation

In this meditation, we focus on our thoughts
   Our brain has the capacity to observe the natural flow of the mind and the contents of our mind. It is called witnessing.
   This process allows us to access a deeper state of mind while building more self-awareness
   It is a simple process
   Close your eyes
   Get comfortable
   Take three deep breaths to ground you and to stop rushing
   Inhale ...
   Exhale ...
   Inhale ...
   Exhale ...
   Now, begin observing your individual thoughts
   Witnessing has three steps
   You observe the individual thought
   You label them
   And you let go
   so, you can dive deep into the still and silent consciousness
   Beyond the mind and its thinking process
   It might seem hard
   But it's really not
   The more you can become witness to your thoughts
   The less control the thoughts have over you
   Increasing your freedom of choice
   It also weakens the deep habit patterns that block you from being mindful

As usual, be patient and kind
You can do this as a sitting practice to cultivate the mind
But you can access this at any time you need to
Again, witnessing thoughts does not mean suppression or repression
Just observation
Observe your thought
What is going on?
Label the thoughts
Are they useful?
Or not useful?
When you label a thought not useful, it is not being negative about your own thoughts or about you or your thought process
It is naming the thought pattern for what it is
If it is a positive thought, it is a positive thought
If you have a positive thought, a useful thought, acknowledge it
If you are labeling your thought not useful, then do nothing
Just let it go
No guilt or judgement just let go of a thought that doesn't serve you well
Positive thoughts lead you in the direction of growth
Remind yourself while you continue to practice this
You will find it becomes non-verbal, it becomes easier to differentiate between thoughts
Just say the words internally
Thoughts come
And thoughts go
Your mind is awake when you witness your own thought process
This is a way to train your own mind
To see whether your thought is useful or not useful
This is how you move from your body to conscious mind to unconscious mind
It is about self-observation
Identify and label your individual thought
We cannot really escape our mind
So, witness it
Face your thought process
You are not your thoughts
You can observe them
As usual, in all mindful practice
You have to find out for yourself
Try it
And own your truth
What kind of thoughts are in your own mind right now?
Knowing where your mind is now tells you how to get where you're going

Are you disturbed?
If you are disturbed or restless, or troubled or wandering
You could characterize that and label
I am severely disturbed
I am mildly distracted
Or you could be in a dull state of mind
Or you could be distracted
Your mind is flitting from here to there
When you see your own thoughts and your own mind
You understand
When you are attracted to something
Or you are averse to something
Just bring your mind
Observe, label
Even if you continue to be distracted, it is okay
Just be aware of your own state of mind
What are you thinking right now?
Can you observe your own mind?
And see what you are thinking
Label it
Can you move from a disturbing or distracted thought to a more light,
illuminated, and positive action-oriented one?
If your mind is overly active or noisy, you want to allow that to pass
To transform to clarity and illumination
If your mind is clear, you want to gently maintain the state of mind
If your mind is heavy, acknowledge it
Label it
You want to move towards lightness
It is not good or bad
It is useful or not useful
Another question you can ask is:
Is this particular thought colored or not colored?
What is a colored thought?
Colored thoughts have a negative valence
They have a disturbing quality
You might have an emotional attraction to one or other
You might be attracted
Or you might have an aversion
So, if the thought is not connected to I or Me, that usually means it is a
colored thought
The not colored thought is a neutral thought
That means you are not attached to it
It is just data
And you are not reactive

Sometimes through practice
Your previously colored thoughts have may have lost some of the coloring
That means you have developed a neutral attitude to that thought
So simply observe the individual thought
That flows in the stream of your mind
Rises and falls
And ask yourself
Literally ask yourself
Is this thought colored or not colored?
The goal is to train your mind by internally labelling it
So, a thought arises
You ask, is this thought colored or not colored?
Maybe the answer is, "colored"
Then ask yourself, is this thought useful or not useful
If the answer is not useful, then train your mind
You can tell your mind
"This thought is not useful, you can either let go, explore or cultivate the thought"
This may be a slow process, but it builds up over time
If your current thought is colored and not useful
You can let go of it or you can explore it further
Why is the thought colored?
What valence does it have for me?
If your thought is colored and useful, then you might tell yourself
Yes, this is a good idea, I might pursue this further
If the thought is not colored or mildly colored
Usually the thought itself drifts away
You are intentionally allowing a thought to arise
Let the thought arise
Observe it and then label it
Is it useful?
Not useful?
When you can neutrally witness the entire stream of your thoughts
It is easier to examine individual thought patterns
Then it is easier to go beyond the mind towards the consciousness
The original thought may stay but it might lose its coloring
Its attraction or repulsion
So sometimes the previously troublesome thoughts would become mere memories
Because you can observe them
Then you can ask
Is it a correct thought?
Is it an accurate perception?

Am I seeing the thought clearly?
Is it coming from an uncluttered mind?
Or are there other things in my mind making it hazy?
It could be an inaccurate perception
Incorrect knowledge
Crowded thinking
You can also ask yourself if this thought is a fantasy
An imagery
Sometimes your thoughts come from memories
So, observe if your perceptions are clear or crowded
If your mind is fantasizing or drifting to sleep
Or is it just mere streams from our memory?
The store house of impressions we all have
You want to cultivate the capacity to see with clarity
And the first step is to observe your individual thought
So, observe your thoughts
One thought at a time
Label it
Is it useful? Or not useful?
Is it colored? Or not colored?
Is it clear? Or hazy?
Should I act on this? Or should I let this go?
You want to remind yourself
Stay awake, stay alert
How can I be fully present and see clearly?
You want to cultivate clear thinking
You want to cultivate correct perception
You want to seek a convergence
To get into the space of flow
It is a psychological state
You can bring it with you to everyday life
Your day-to-day thoughts
Understanding the source of your thoughts
Understanding your own reactions
Understanding if you are clear thinking or hazy thinking
As usual be gentle on yourself
You can practice this any time
You can ask yourself this question any time of the day
And observe your thought
Now open your eyes gently

******

Daily Activity: What Is Your Core Identity? – Part I

How much do you identify with the following? Use a five-point scale (1 – not at all to 5 – very much)

- Your immediate family
- Your organizational affiliation (work, church, volunteer, sports, etc.)
- Your community (local, geographic, ethnic, racial)
- Your compatriots – fellow country men and women
- All of humanity
- All of universe including the planet and all the living things

Did your perception change from the previous time you did this? Why or why not?

Journal Prompt

If you are doing the thoughts-based meditation after a while, how did it feel? Do you still feel the same way the first time you tried it? How was your practice? What is your cognitive response to core identity exercise?

Day 18

Emotions Meditation

In this meditation, we are going to focus on our emotions
We are always sitting on emotions
They are our foreground and our background
But we hardly ever pay attention to them
Self-awareness is knowing our emotional state and being able to identify it
That is what we are going to do today
Sit comfortably
Close your eyes
Take three deep breaths
In and out
Pay special attention to your abdomen and lungs
You can even touch them
Place one hand on your abdomen and one hand on your chest
Feel them expand
In and out
One more time
In and out
Now, pay attention to what you are feeling
What is your emotional state right now?
Take a little time

Guessing is okay
A lot of times we don't know what we are feeling exactly
But to know that we are feeling some kind of emotion is actually good
It is a good starting point
A lot of times we don't know
So, pay attention to your emotion
You can feel a lot of emotions
Painful or pleasant
Delight or joy or happiness or gratitude or love or hopefulness or optimism or empathy
It could also be negative
You could be frustrated with this whole thing
You could be irritated with this practice and feel a certain resistance
Or you could be anxious about it
Or about something that is coming up
Or you could even be feeling aversion sometimes
That happens
And that is okay
But you are just going to sit and acknowledge that emotion
You identify that emotion
The most important thing is that you identify the emotion, not identify with it
That means you don't act out on it
The emotion doesn't become you
You, your brain, your mind, your thought process can see the emotion
That is identify *and not* identify with *your emotion*
It is something that is passing through you even if it is longer term
When you can identify your emotion
The next thing you can do is to identify your emotion's location in your body
A lot of times, our bodies give us the clues
Even when we are not aware of our own emotions, our body gives us the clues and sometimes it outright screams
If you are anxious and pretending not to be, you might feel a gripping, tightening or burning sensation
For lot of people, stress goes to their shoulders or neck or stomach
For many, anxiety goes to the stomach as well
Butterflies in the stomach
Good excitement, anticipation
Sometimes it is too much
It is churning because we are nervous
We are making the body, mind, emotion connection
Pay attention
Where are we feeling it?

Sometimes we feel kind of nervous and we want to giggle
To release the tension
Or you have energy, you want to rock or move because you are not comfortable with the stillness
The discomfort with stillness could just be boredom
Why am I sitting to observe the emotion?
I have no emotion I am just bored
So, observe the boredom
A lot of the time emotions manifest as bodily pain or symptoms, psychosomatic
Your body is as much engaged in the emotions as your mind is
So, identify your emotions
Just observe them
Even knowing that you are feeling something is okay
So what are you feeling?
Where is it sitting in your body?
Maybe right now you are getting impatient or irritated with this meditation
That is okay
Just pay attention to the impatience and irritation
You don't even have to ask why
We all have a range of emotional life
Sometimes it is disgust
Sometimes it is adoration
Just identify
Stay with it
Feel the feeling
Sheer awareness puts you outside of your comfort zone
Just acknowledging it puts you out of your comfort zone
Can you step out of your comfort zone?
Can you be open to that?
Be with the emotion
Show a mirror
Shine a light
Can you be present to your own emotions?
A gentle gaze on your emotion
Not judgment
Whatever you are feeling is valid because you're feeling it
Positive or negative
Anything you are feeling is legitimate
You don't have to legitimize it
You don't have to explain it
A gentle gaze
A gentle curiosity

A gentle compassion to yourself
The cause of the emotion is irrelevant
You don't have to ask "why am I feeling this way?"
That is not important in this context
Just feel the feelings
Feel it in your body
Develop self-awareness about your emotions
Let go of the idea about the emotions
The why is irrelevant
It is the what
Can you actually identify it?
Do you know what you are feeling?
Can you stay with it?
Can you go to the place of deep stillness?
Where you can be comfortable with yourself
And watch yourself
What is going on?
Bring your focus gently to your emotions
You have the tools to do it
You know how to do breathing meditation
You know how to do body scan
You are finding another layer
You are combining body scan
Looking for where your emotion sits
Where does it show up in your body?
You feel it you will know before you feel it
Because your body tells you
Your body is deeply tied to your brain
Your experiences, your memories, and your emotions
So, you are establishing a connection between your emotions and your body
How do they go together?
Your body becomes an instrument for you to understand
It is another clue to your emotional landscape map
It tells your where your stress sits
You feel happy or sad or stressed or frustrated or bored
How does your body act?
Just staying with the emotions
That is a gift
Even if you are irritable, that is okay
Just paying attention
Paying attention to your emotions and its connections to your physical body
You don't have to deal with more than you have to

The key is to be strong, patient, and consistent
Sometimes this practice can open up memories and emotions
You just feel them with no conditions, no judgment
Just unconditional acceptance of your own feelings
No judgment
If you feel jealous, you feel jealous
If you are angry, you are angry
If you are happy, you are happy
You don't have to ask why
You don't have to explain it
You just have to identify it
And be with it
To identify it right now, you must be present in the moment
You can't describe a past feeling
You can't describe a future feeling
You only describe a memory when you are describing the past
Be with it right now
Take a couple of deep breaths
In and out
In and out
Open your eyes very gently

******

Daily Activity: What Is Your Core Identity? – Part 2

When they are in need, how much do you want to help? Use a five-point scale (1 – not at all to 5 – very much)
- Your family
- Your organizational affiliation (work, church, volunteer, sports, etc.)
- Your community (local, geographic, ethnic, racial)
- Your compatriots – fellow country men and women
- All of humanity
- All of universe including the planet and all the living things.

Did your perception change from the previous time you did this? Why or why not?

Journal Prompt

If you are doing the emotions-based meditation after a while, how did it feel? Do you still feel the same way the first time you tried it? How was your practice? What is your emotional response to core identity exercise?

Day 19

Going Back to Gratitude Meditation

In this practice, we focus on gratitude. It is always a good time to practice gratitude. There is no better time than now to practice gratitude. Sometimes, in the busyness of life, we forget to be thankful.

Close your eyes. Take three deep breaths.

In and out
In and out
In and out
I want you to bring your awareness to things in your life for which you are thankful
When you identify the first thing you are thankful for, just let it sink in
Let yourself sink into the feeling and surrender
Notice how it feels in your body
First, be grateful for your breath
Bring your awareness to the breath
As you inhale and as you exhale and the fact that your breath is life
Breath is life
It keeps you alive
Then become aware of your heart
It is strong
It is resilient
It beats all the time
It is beating, it is pulsing, filling with love, filling with blood
And peace and flowing it all back out
Bring your awareness to your eyes
That let you see colors, smiles, nature, the sunrise, the sunset
The rainbow, the moon, and the stars, and yourself in the mirror
Bring your awareness to your ears
That lets you hear the sound
Music, laughter, the voice of loved ones, the silence, and the beautiful sounds of life
Then focus on your nose
The smells, the ocean breeze brings, the sweet perfume of flowers, of newly cut grass
The smells wafting from the kitchen
Now focus on your lips, and your mouth, and your tongue
That tastes, savors, and nourishes
Kisses and speaks, and whispers and sings
Next, bring your awareness to your hands
That hold and touch and hug
That open and close and squeeze

The arms and shoulders that hug and carry and lift and stretch
Our feet, our toes, the gift to wiggle them
Transporting you, walk, run, dangle, dance, kick, leap, and point
Be thankful for your body
It is the only house you have in this world
What about your emotions?
Your joy
Your sorrow
The strength that helps you make it through every day
Say thank you to your emotions
That guide you
That shape you
Then bring your awareness to your abundance, your expansion, your
evolution
Your perspective shifts
The affluence, and flow, and empathy, love and light
And your ability to see growth and potential in every moment
We live in the best time in human history
You are everything you need
Be grateful
Say thank you to your life, your body, and your emotions
Now, breathe
Feel more grace and ease
Experience the warmth, love and compassion that being thankful brings
to your heart
Next, drift your awareness to nurturing relationships in your life
New ones
Older ones
Old friends, family, new friends, your teachers
Your coaches, your partners, your teammates
Say thank you to all the good people in your life
And even those who seem bad at times but give you an opportunity to
learn and grow
And stretch your love, your compassion, your empathy
Breathe in ...
And breathe out ...
Send thanks for the material things that come to you unexpectedly
Or things you worked hard for
With great effort, commitment, and hard work
Say thank you to the things that give you comfort, convenience, ease of life
And joy
Think of all the love you have in your life
Your connection to those who are sweet, loving, and honorable and feel
right

That connect you to deep inside yourself as well as outside of you
When we no longer take life for granted, we become grateful for everything that we have
Just breathe and feel the flow of gratitude
It is always a season for thankfulness
We are blessed with a lot of things
Even if at the moment we feel anxious about the transitions, about the future
Even if we feel guilt or shame about the past
We are still standing
We are breathing
We are surrounded by people who love and whom we love
We are surrounded by beauty
We are surrounded by abundance
And we are standing
We are breathing
Let the gratitude, thankfulness for your life, for your body, for your heart, your things, your people, your ideas, your accomplishments, your success, your opportunities for growth and learning flow through you
Be thankful for all of them and let the gratitude fill your body, your heart
See how it feels
Take deep breaths and when you are satisfied, gently open your eyes

******

Daily Activity: What Is Your Core Identity? – Part 3

Who do you donate most to? Use a five-point scale (1-not at all to 5 – most)

- What, donate? I work hard to protect my family's financial security and future.
- Your organization – alumni organization, church, etc.
- Your community – local food bank, local charities, your ethnic group associations, etc.
- National philanthropic organizations – United Way, etc.
- International Red Cross and other international relief and rescue organizations, fundraising campaigns for private individuals you do not know.
- Animal shelters, Nature Conservancy, etc.

From the first time you did this exercise to now, has anything shifted about your core identity?

Journal Prompt

What are you grateful for? Who are you grateful for?

Day 20

Ideal Self in Community

In this meditation, we are going to try and develop a picture of what your ideal or highest self in the context of your chosen, beloved community.

As usual, we begin with the breath and commit to kindness and compassion to self. It is easy to focus on the gaps between who we wish to be and how we show up right now, but we want to focus on our highest aspirations for ourselves.

Take three deep grounding breaths
Breathe in ...
Breathe out ...
Breathe in ...
Breathe out ...
Breathe in ...
Breathe out ...
Now connect to your entire body
Ground in your body
Feel who you are
From head to toe
Feel the oxygen pulsing through your body
Its every cell
Feel being open, confident, kind, and joyful
Open to possibilities, opportunities, responsibilities
Bring to mind your immediate circle of relationships
Partner, child, parent, friends, and family
How do you show up with them?
What is your ideal self in this circle of intimates?
This is your relational ideal self
Breathe in ...
Breathe out ...
Breathe in ...
Breathe out ...
What kind of partner or parent or child do you want to be?
Sibling and friend
How do you want to be seen by this group of people?
Can you see them being proud of you?
Can you see what their needs are?
Can you see how they need you to show up?

What would it take for you to show up in that way?
Breathe in ...
Breathe out ...
Breathe in ...
Breathe out ...
Breathe in ...
Breathe out ...
Now expand your circle beyond your immediate friends and family
Consider other groups you belong to
Or organizations you are part of
Or maybe your work
Who are these people?
What are the value alignments between you and them?
Do they give you purpose?
Do they give you energy? Affirmation for your personhood?
What kind of commitment do you feel towards them?
How do you show up for these groups and people?
How do they need you to show up?
What would it take for you to show up in that way?
Breathe in ...
Breathe out ...
Breathe in ...
Breathe out ...
Breathe in ...
Breathe out ...
How do you show up for your community?
How do they need you to show up?
How would you like to show up and be seen by them?
Breathe in ...
Breathe out ...
Breathe in ...
Breathe out ...
Breathe out ...
And open your eyes gently when you are ready

******

Daily Activity: Embedded-Self Exercise

You will need a stack of post-it notes and an empty wall or newsprint for this exercise.

- Step 1: Take a piece of paper and a pen
- Step 2: Write on top "I am ..."

- Step 3: Set a timer for 60 seconds
- Step 4: Complete the sentence with as many words as you can.
- Step 5: Now write each word on separate post-it notes.
- Step 6: Divide the wall or newsprint into three columns.
- Step 7: Title the three columns "Who am I now?" "Who was I before?" "Who will I become?"
- Step 8: How does your past influence your present and future? How does the vision of your future influence your present?

These are your time embedded identity systems.

Journal Prompt: Boundary Management

How do you manage your boundaries between your individual, inter-personal, and tribal identities? Do you sometimes feel overwhelmed by the demands placed on you from other people and organizations you belong to? Do you sometimes feel hesitant to ask for help or support? Are you good at boundary setting? Can you think of an example of when you felt effective at boundary setting without burning a bridge? Can you think of a time when you felt that you worked across the boundaries well while serving individual, relational, and tribal/organizational needs? What would you like to improve on?

Day 21

Loving Kindness Meditation

Settle into the awareness of the body and the breath
  Breathe in ...
  Breathe out ...
  Breathe in ...
  Breathe out ...
  After you have connected with the breath
  Feel your body
  Noticing what is there
  Connect your breath to body
  Breathe in ...
  Breathe out ...
  Be open to whatever you can experience in the moment, in the body
  Feel the breath moving through your heart
  We first begin with loving kindness towards ourselves
  Allowing our heart to open with tenderness
  Remember your basic goodness
  Maybe you want to remember a time when you were kind or generous

And your natural desire to be happy and not to suffer
If you are finding it difficult to acknowledge your own goodness
Look at yourself through the eyes of someone who loves you
What does that person love about you?
Or you may recall the unconditional love that you felt from your pet
And some of us find it hard
If you find it even harder
Use your imagination and picture yourself as a young child
Feel the tender feelings that you would feel towards this young child
As you experience this love
Notice how you feel in your body
Maybe you feel warm or some heat or a smile
Or a sense of expansiveness
This is loving kindness
A natural feeling that is accessible to all of us
Rest for a few moments with this feeling
Of open and unconditional love for yourself
Bask in that loving kindness towards yourself
Breathe in ...
Breathe out ...
What does it feel like to feel the acceptance?
Now, make a wish for yourself
May I be happy
May I be peaceful
May I be held in loving kindness
May I feel filled with loving kindness
May I feel centered and calm
May I feel connected and calm
May I know the natural joy of being alive
May I be safe
May I be peaceful and at ease
If there are feelings of warmth or friendliness or love in your body or mind
Connect to them
Allow them to grow
Direct the loving kindness to yourself
Then bring to mind a friend or someone in your life who has deeply cared for you
And send your loving kindness to them
May you be happy
May you be well
May you be safe and peaceful
May you be the recipient of loving kindness
May you be filled with loving kindness
Sink into the intention and the heartfelt feeling you have for this person

They have done so much for you
You feel love for them
Affection, warmth, acceptance
Feel the feelings and send them your good intentions
Connect the feelings to the phrases
As you continue, open the circle to someone that is neutral
You may see them regularly but not know them well
They could be a neighbor
Someone at the store
Somebody that you know of, but you don't know well
Bring this person to your mind now
And use the same phrases
May you be happy
May you be well
May you be safe
May you be peaceful and at ease
May you receive loving kindness
May you be filled with loving kindness
Sometimes during this meditation you might even feel the opposite feelings
Anger, grief, or sadness
That is a good sign that your heart is softening
Accept that with whatever patience and kindness you can muster for the same feelings
Instead, direct loving kindness towards them
Now bring to mind someone with whom you have had a difficult relationship
Perhaps it is someone you find difficult to like or feel compassion
This is the time to remind yourself that this person is a whole being
They also need loving kindness
As someone who may feel pain and anxiety
As someone who may suffer
As someone as human as you are
See if it is possible to extend the words of loving kindness to these people or this person
May you be safe
May you be happy
May you feel my love now
May you feel loving kindness
May you be filled with loving kindness
Now allow your awareness to spread in all directions
Imagine that you are standing in a vast space
That you can connect to everyone and everything
Yourself, people whom you love
People to whom you feel neutral
People to whom you feel negative

All human beings, all animals
The rich tapestry of the universe
With all the prospects for joy and sorrow,
War and peace
Hunger, abundance
Love, joy, anger, everything that composes your mind and the world
And now, send the loving kindness to everyone and everything
May you be safe
May you be happy
May you feel loving kindness
May you be filled with loving kindness
May all beings be filled with loving kindness
May all beings be happy
May all beings be awakened and free
May all beings be safe
Now, come back to yourself and see how you feel
If you feel the love and the warmth in your body
In your heart, in your face
Sometimes it is even in the toes
Bask in the energy of loving kindness that you have generated
And the people that practice this all over the world have generated
Connect back to your breath
Breathe in ...
Breathe out ...
Breathe in ...
Breathe out ...
Enjoy the feeling
Breathe in ...
Breathe out ...
Take this moment to connect with yourself and with the universe
With love and kindness and compassion
And gently open your eyes

******

Daily Activity: Counterfactual Thinking – What If This Is Not Your Community?

- Step 1: Pick one community salient to your identity.
- Step 2: Now, ask a counterfactual question: what if you did not belong to that community? How would that have changed you? How would your identity have shifted? How would your life story have shifted?
- Step 3: What did you learn from this exercise?

Journal Prompt

Reflect on your relationship with the different nexus of embeddedness. By being less tribal and more expansive, what would you gain? What would you lose?

Notes

1 https://nativegov.org/a-guide-to-indigenous-land-acknowledgment.
2 https://www.smithsonianmag.com/history/true-native-new-yorkers-can-never-tru
   ly-reclaim-their-homeland-180970472/#:~:text=When%20the%20Dutch%20arriv
   ed%20in,amicable%2C%20according%20to%20historical%20records.&text=As
   %20the%20myth%20goes%2C%20the,from%20the%20Lenape%20in%201626.

Chapter 15

Expansive-Universal Self
(Days 22–28)

In this part of the journey, for the next seven days, you will examine your expansive identity system and related mental models and close on Day 28.

Table 15.1 Week 4

Day	Meditation	To-do	Journal Prompt
22	Reciprocity	Your Identity Tree Exercise	What part of your identity do you struggle with most? How can you bring compassion and acceptance to those parts?
23	Self-Compassion		What is in your compost? What resentments do you hold due to your identities? How do you bring sympathetic joy to those who have hurt you, victimized you, or made you feel weak?
24	Sympathetic Joy		What does the world give to you? What do you want to give to the world?
25	Guilt to Gratitude and Generosity		What parts of your identity and life make you feel guilty? How do you atone for them? How can you convert your guilt into gratitude and generosity?
26	Gift-giving	Leadership Philosophy and Integrative Mental Models	When was the last time you gave a gift to someone you loved? Or someone you didn't even know? How does gift-giving make you feel?
27	Ideal Self in the Universe		How do you manage your boundaries between your individual, inter-personal, and tribal identities?
28	Loving Kindness		Who are you?

Day 22

Reciprocity Meditation

*In this meditation, we are going to focus on giving and receiving —
reciprocity*
   Give and take is the root of relationships
   *It is done to develop our compassion, our kindness, and open up our
being to kindness*
   Take a comfortable position
   Close your eyes
   And focus on your breathing
   Breathe in ...
   Breathe out ...
   *When you give and receive, you begin to be open, and accept others and
yourself in a more kind, and understanding way*
   Open your mind to receiving help
   People are willing to invest in you
   Asking for help is the biggest advocacy action you can do for yourself
   Think of the people and the loving and supportive relationships in your life
   Those who are willing to support your growth
   Be a cheerleader
   A facilitator
   Mentors and sounding boards
   As you inhale
   Accept the help
   During exhalation
   Send your well wishes to those who are giving you the help
   Send your gratitude to those who are willing to help
   You can do both
   Deeply and lightly
   Inhale ...
   Exhale ...
   Imagine that you are breathing through every cell of your body
   And your cells have permeable boundaries
   *Inhale the warmth, compassion, support, love, affection, and the regard
from those closest to you*
   Those who support you
   Those who want the best for you
   And as you breathe out
   You give the same affection, love, support and consideration to them
   Reciprocity
   To give and take
   Receiving requires humility

Understanding that you cannot do everything by yourself
That you need help
Asking for help is standing up for yourself
But also practicing humility
A lot of us are trained to be strong, independent
With steel in our spine
I invite you to melt that steel
Be a river that flows
Be light that refracts rather than an unmoving, immobile spine of steel
Humility and mercy
Humility and compassion
Humility to receive
To ask for help and to receive it
Bring to your mind the person who is on the top of your list
Feel the connection with them
They may be your child, your parent, your friend, your grandmother
Your teacher
Your spouse, your partner
Be one with them
Send them love
May you be safe
May you be healthy
May you never be separated from great happiness
And receive their love
Their affection
Their regard for you
When you receive their love
You melt that steel
You don't need that steel
People that love you and support are part of your being
Send a deep, cool, spacious, healing breath to your friend
Let the outbreath pour through every pore of your body
Breathe out spaciousness, openness, kindness, and surrender
Breathe in love and affection that comes from people closest to you
Breathe in ...
And breathe out ...
Say thank you
To those who have helped you
To those who you know will help you
As the hardness dissolves, your heart gets more alive
With humility you get support
Imagine this person sitting right across from you
Both of you have your eyes closed
And you are connecting through your hearts

Breathe in ...
Breathe out ...
Imagine your breath is synchronized with theirs
You are connected
Your heartbeats regulate each other's
Be a breathing presence for all beings
As you sit across from your friend
Breathe in ...
Breathe out ...
Notice your feelings, your fears, your ego
But remember the depth of your commitment to them and their commitment to your well-being
Breathe in ...
Breathe out ...
Stay in the moment
When you are ready
Let your mind's eye rise to meet the eye of the friend sitting across from you
Be present
Gaze into the eyes of your friend
Let your good heart connect with their good heart
There is shared humanity in suffering and greatness
Connect with that humanity in that person who is present for you
Be with this person
Close your eyes
And focus on your breath
Imagine this person as a child
They probably had the same dreams you had
They probably needed the same kind of help you needed
Breathe in ...
Breathe out ...
They are your friend, your parent, your child, your partner
Breathe in ...
Breathe out ...
Your heart of compassion is wide open
Your heart of humility is wide open
To receive help and to give help
Give and take
Breathe in love
Breathe out kindness
Breathe in love
Breathe out kindness
Now, open the focus of your practice to the universe
Breathe in universal suffering and compassion
Dissolving your own self-importance and ego

Give away all your goodness to all beings
Giving and receiving is one of the richest and bravest practices that we can do
Giving requires mercy and compassion
Receiving requires humility and self-compassion
Breathe in ...
Breathe out ...
Cultivate these relationships
Not instrumentally
But by genuine compassion
By giving you will receive
By asking you will give them the gift, the joy of them giving you something
In a reciprocal relationship, the gift of giving and receiving, both are there
Sometimes they need something from you
But it is okay
You can pay it forward
You can receive
There are no rules
Except humility and compassion
Breathe in ...
Breathe out ...
The people in your list
They are your cheerleaders
Your witnesses
As you pursue your life, your vision, your goals and dreams
Bow your head to your heart
For such relationships are of the heart
Breathe in ...
Breathe out ...
Thank them for holding you in their circle
A circle of affection, warmth, friendship, fellowship
Giving you kindness and compassion
In the next exhalation, you send your love, friendship, kindness, and compassion
Giving and receiving
Reciprocity
Breathe in ...
Breathe out ...
Take your time to open your eyes slowly
Breathe in ...
Breathe out ...

******

Daily Activity: Your Identity Tree (inspired by The Tree of Life work by David Denborough[1] and Ncazelo Ncube)

The Tree of Life exercise was developed as a psychotherapy tool and integrates cultural differences and identities to process one's life through narratives. I find this a powerful tool to explore our identities. Identities are created, sustained, and propagated through stories too; stories we tell ourselves, stories we tell others, and stories we tell each other. Today, you will complete one part of it.

Your Identity Tree – Part I

Take a deep breath. Sit or stand comfortably anchored by your beautiful feet to the ground.

Close your eyes if you haven't already done so.

Take three deep breaths to clear your mind.

Inhale ... Exhale ...

Inhale ... Exhale ...

Inhale ... Exhale ...

Repeat after me:

I promise to engage in this contemplative practice fully, mindfully, thoughtfully, heartfully, and non-judgmentally. I believe that we all can learn and grow. Our identities can shift shape with time and knowledge. I will be open to such change.

Now open your eyes.

Take a piece of paper and a pen or pencil and draw a tree.

You don't need to be an artist to draw a tree. Just draw a figure that resembles a tree.

The roots: What are the influences? Where do you come from? Your town? Your village? Your family history? Treasured traditions? Ancestors? People who taught you, influenced you when you were a child?

The ground: What anchors you? What nourishes you? What makes you feel safe, grounded, and steady?

Save your work.

Journal Prompt

What does the world give to you? What do you want to give to the world?

Day 23

Self-Compassion Meditation

This meditation will focus on self-acceptance and self-compassion

Find a comfortable position and notice how you are sitting or standing
Notice how you are feeling physically and mentally
Take a deep breath in through your nose
And out through mouth
Take another breath
And allow your breathing to relax you as you exhale fully
Breathe in gently
As you breathe out, let the air carry your tension out of the body
Continue to breathe slowly and gently
As you begin to focus on relaxing your body
Notice where your body is tense
Focus your attention there
As you breathe, picture that part of your body as slightly more relaxed than before
With each breath, that part of your body becomes a little more relaxed
Imagine what the relaxation feels like
Soft, gentle, calm, loose, free, and let that relaxation feeling grow
Scan your body for any areas of tension
For each area, let the relaxing breath soften the muscle as they give up their hold
Let the feeling of relaxation grow
Spreading calm throughout your body
Breathe in relaxation
Breathe out tension
Let all the tension go as you exhale
Continue to breathe slowly and gently
Deepening your state of relaxation
More and more
With each breath
Deeper and deeper
More and more relaxed
Calm and at peace
Now, begin to create a picture in your mind
Imagine a place where you feel completely at ease
A place you have been
A place you may have seen
Or completely imaginary
Picture this place where you feel happy and calm
Create the details about this place in your mind
Visualize the sights, smells, and sounds of your place
Imagine how you feel physically
Enjoying being still or relaxing
Or whatever enjoyable activities you engage there
Enjoy the way you feel safe in this place

You feel calm and safe here
At peace with yourself
Remain in your peaceful place
While you meditate and build your self esteem
Imagine all the following affirmations are true for you
Right now, in this moment, enjoy the self-esteem relaxation in your mind
Repeat each affirmation after me with conviction
Use your imagination to fully believe the self-esteem relaxation affirmations
I am at peace with myself
I appreciate who I am
I value myself as a person
All people have value
I am a valuable human being
I deserve to relax
I deserve to be happy
I embrace my happy feelings
I embrace being content
I imagine and believe that all of these affirmations are true for me and enjoy the self-affirmation relaxation that I am experiencing
When my mood is low, I accept my emotions and recognize that the low mood will pass, and I will be happy again
I look forward to the good times
My future is bright and positive
I look forward to the future and enjoy the present
I look back fondly at many memories from the past
I forgive myself for my mistakes
All people make mistakes
I used to feel regret for some of my mistakes because I am a good person and I always want to do the best I can
And now, I have learned, and I have moved on
I am still a good person
I have released the feelings of regrets
I forgive myself for errors that I have made
Because I have felt bad long enough for them
I have suffered enough and now it is time to be free
By freeing myself from past mistakes, I can move on and do good things
I forgive myself
I believe that all these affirmations are true in this moment
I feel good about who I am today
I accept my flaws and I accept myself
I view my shortcomings as strengths not yet developed rather than weaknesses
I eagerly develop my strengths

I imagine and believe that all of these affirmations are true for me in this moment

I approach challenges with strength and not anxiety

I do my best at that time

I also accept my imperfections in what I do

My efforts are good enough and they are okay

I do not have to be perfect to be a good person

I am a human being with flaws

I enjoy being who I am

I nurture the child within me

I feel secure with who I am and do not need to compare myself with others

All the strengths I have heard are present in me today

I still have the same positive character even if not all my strengths are shown right now

I have all those strengths of character and will use them again

I imagine and believe that all these affirmations are true for me right now

I accept myself

I care for myself

I take time for myself and enjoy it.

I deserve time for myself

I feel good about taking this time regularly

I handle difficulties with grace

I allow myself to experience and express emotions, both positive and negative

I accept myself

I am perfect the way I am, and I accept myself

I am a valuable human being

I feel confident

I accept myself

I feel secure

I accept myself

Think again of your peaceful place

Picture yourself enjoying the place accepting the affirmations

Any positive feelings or negative feelings, you can still feel calm and at peace

Now it is time to leave your special place but know that you can return to it at any time when you need to

Take with you the feelings of self-compassion, self-esteem and continue to feel positive

Hold onto these positive feelings of acceptance as you return to your day

In a moment, I will count to three and increase your alertness and you will become fully awake on the third count

One

Take a deep cleansing breath and exhale

Two

Take a deep breath and exhale
Three
You are feeling calm, refreshed and confident

******

Daily Activity: Your Identity Tree – Part 2

Take a deep breath. Sit or stand comfortably anchored by your beautiful feet to the ground. Close your eyes if you haven't already done so. Take three deep breaths to clear your mind.

Inhale ... Exhale ...
Inhale ... Exhale ...
Inhale ... Exhale ...

Repeat after me:

I promise to engage in this contemplative practice fully, mindfully, thoughtfully, heartfully, and non-judgmentally. I believe that we all can learn and grow. Our identities can shift shape with time and knowledge. I will be open to such change.

Now open your eyes. Pick up your work from yesterday and add the following.

The branches: What are the current organizational groups and systems you belong to? These can include professional affiliations, religious or community groups, family groups, etc. What part of your identity does each branch provide?

The leaves: Each leaf should represent a key person or relationship in your life. What does that look like? What do these relationships reveal about your identity?

The fruits: What have you accomplished in recent years? Ideas? Things or organizations you created? What do these tell you about your identity?

The seeds: What do you want your legacy to be? If your tree is crowded, please feel free to plant the seeds in the ground.

Journal Prompt

What part of your identity do you struggle with most? How can you bring compassion and acceptance to those parts?

Day 24

Universal Sympathetic Joy

In this meditation, we are going to try cultivating sympathetic joy
Sympathetic joy is being happy at somebody else's happiness

Feeling joy at someone else's good fortune
It is one of the most difficult concepts and practices
Because we are so conditioned to compare ourselves with others
So conditioned to treat the world as a competitive space
So someone's good fortune, someone's accomplishments
Something that makes someone else happy
Feels like it is diminishing us somehow.
It is also because we are so used to feeling inadequate
Feeling less than
Because when the world is organized by hierarchy
Someone is better than the other
Someone is on top of another
And also, because we see this as a divided world
Because we don't see ourselves as one with the universe
We see ourselves as divided and separate
If that is the way the world is perceived, it is difficult to feel joy at someone else's happiness
Because they are not us
We are not happy
It is their happiness
This is kind of conditioned
Sympathetic is the opposite of jealousy and envy
Envy and jealousy come from comparisons, division, inadequacy
Seeing, even momentarily, everyone as separate versus one makes it hard to be happy at someone else's happiness
But we are one
By Mother Earth
Whose big breath gives us all breath, life
The prince and the pauper
The oppressed and the oppressor
The saint and the scoundrel
We are all part of the same tapestry
When we share in someone else's joy, we feel part of their happiness
And for that one moment at least, we are not separate from them
We are going to try and feel that
And take joy at other people's joy
As usual, we start with the breath
Take a comfortable position
Close your eyes
Take three deep, delicious, and generous breaths that connect us to the universe and Mother Earth's breath
Breathe in ...
Breathe out ...
Breathe in ...

Breathe out ...
Breathe in ...
Breathe out ...
For good measure, because sympathetic joy is a bit difficult to feel for many of us, let's take one more deep breath
Breathe in ...
Breathe out ...
Now think of a time when you were happy
So happy
It could be something very small
It could be something very big
The trigger itself doesn't matter
It is the happiness you felt
Bring to mind your beautiful face when you are happy
What does your face look like?
How does it feel in your face?
Do you feel warm?
Do you feel flushed in your face?
How does it feel?
Experience that moment
Bring to your mind a moment of happiness
How does it feel in your face?
In your body?
In your heart
Now, think of someone that you know feels happiness at your joy, your success
Think of someone who is most happy with your good news
That friend, that parent, that teacher, a mentor, or partner
Who feels joy at your joy?
Bring to your mind their face
How do they react to your happiness in the moment?
What does their face look like when they are so happy for you?
Does their face beam with happiness for you?
Does their face radiate generosity of spirit?
Imprint that on your mind
How do you feel when someone is happy for you?
And it shows
How does it make you feel?
Grateful? More happy?
Say thank you for sharing in your joy
Thank you for doubling your happiness because you reflect it back.
Say thank you to the universe for giving this person to you in that moment
Someone that cheers you, supports you, someone that can show sympathetic joy to you

Now recall a moment when you saw them happy
Which made you happy
Recall how their face shines when they receive your sympathetic joy
When they feel one with you because your happiness mirrors theirs
As we know our brain has mirror neurons that multiply every emotion
Radiant joy at others' happiness
Pay attention to this person's joy because you are happy for them
That is being one in joy
Say thank you to them for giving you an opportunity to share in their joy
Say thank you for giving you a joyful moment
Breathe in ...
Breathe out ...
Breathe in ...
Breathe out ...
Breathe in ...
Breathe out ...
Breathe in ...
Breathe out ...
Breathe in ...
Breathe out ...
Now bring to mind someone with whom you are neutral
Someone with whom you don't have an emotional valence
Not particularly positive or negative
Someone you may see occasionally
Someone you may have not interacted much with
You have no strong feelings for them either way
Imagine them being happy at your happiness
Imagine them responding with positive joy and happiness at your happiness
How does it feel to receive their sympathetic joy?
How does it feel when someone you don't know shows sympathetic joy?
Or someone you know of, but you don't know them in any emotionally meaningful way
How does it feel?
Surprise maybe? Grateful?
You could feel anything
But for this moment, we are not going to focus on the negative emotions you may have
Say suspicion
We are going to focus on the fact that it is delightful, like a surprise
Or gratitude that they are happy for you
That they have generosity of spirit that allows them to be happy
Thank you for surprising me with your positivity and generosity
Your sympathetic joy

Thank you for multiplying my happiness
Thank the universe
Thank you, universe, for giving this moment
This information about how the world can be
Imprint that feeling in your mind
Breathe in ...
Breathe out ...
Breathe in ...
Breathe out ...
Now imagine them being very happy
Maybe you just see them walking down the street
Or in the parking lot
They have a smile on their face
You don't even know what they are happy about
But you smile back and share in their joy
Maybe they got some really good news about their health
Maybe their child got into a college of their choice
Something is going on
Maybe they saw a puppy on the street that made them happy
Maybe they saw a video of a baby panda or cheetah that made them happy
How do you respond?
You know our brain is wired to mirror emotions
You are reflecting their happiness back
For a moment you beam back your joy at seeing them so happy
How does it feel?
And now, say thank you to them for giving you the moment of happiness
Say thank you for sharing your shine and radiance
And multiplying joy and happiness in the world
A moment of joy
Because joy is joy, whether you feel it for yourselves or someone else
Thank you for giving me an opportunity to experience sympathetic joy
Thank you, universe, for sending me someone with such a joyful, happy face
For giving me a moment of joy
Breathe in ...
Breathe out ...
Breathe in ...
Breathe out ...
Breathe in ...
Breathe out ...
Sympathetic joy is even more difficult than compassion
Even compassion to a stranger is easier
We are conditioned to feel compassion
Compassion feeds into the same hierarchical conditioning

Either through our families or religion or societal expectations
Compassion is a feeling, response, action to someone that is in need
Sometimes compassionate response can still come from one up one down
place
Not everyone
It makes us feel good
Yes I am a compassionate person
What we see in our mirror looks good
Compassion makes us feel good and righteous
What we see reflected in the mirror makes us look good
Sympathetic joy is erasing the difference, the separation
It forces us to contend with our dark impulses
Such as jealousy, envy that arises out of our own sense of inadequacy
Society trains us to compare ourselves with others
In a one up one down relationship that disconnects us from each other
As if we are all not part of the same fabric
The same humanity
Then it becomes human tendency to be a bit jealous
because we see others as not ourselves
So, trust your breath to connect to the universal breath
Mother Earth and the trees that nourish us with their big breath
We are all one
The pauper and the prince
The righteous and the rascal
The oppressed and the oppressor
We are all united by our Mother Earth, the life force for all of us
Because she gives us breath, literally
Now take three more deep breaths to cleanse the toxic feelings
Inadequacy, jealousy, comparison with others
Our divisive, divided nature and identity systems
Jealousy is egocentric
Sympathetic joy on the other hand is the rejoicing that we are all one
It is expansive and universal
Breathe in ...
Breathe out ...
Breathe in ...
Breathe out ...
Breathe in ...
Breathe out ...
Breathe in ...
Breathe out ...
Breathe in ...
Breathe out ...
Breathe in ...

Breathe out ...

Now bring to mind someone with whom you don't have a very positive relationship

Not someone with whom we have a very negative relationship

Because that is much more difficult

We are trying to kind and gentle on ourselves

Perhaps your relationship got off on the wrong foot because they said something you didn't care for

Perhaps they misunderstood something you said

Think of that person

Imagine they were happy because you were happy

How do you feel about them now?

What does it feel like to be the recipient of sympathetic joy?

It is possible to feel sympathetic joy with someone with whom we may even have a negative relationship

How does it feel to be the recipient of sympathetic joy?

From a person you did not hold in high esteem or expect to be happy for you

Imagine that they are actually happy for you

How do you feel?

Surprise? Or opening up of your heart?

And willingness to revisit your relationship with them

Or reappraisal of them

Wow, I am pretty shocked

I never expected this from them

I didn't expect them to respond to my happiness

I just didn't expect that!

Maybe I miscalculated

Maybe I am holding on to an idea of them that is stuck in time

Maybe there are parts to them I didn't appreciate or connect with

I did not give them grace, the benefit of the doubt

That is the most reassuring thing about the universe

About your fellow humans

That even the ones we didn't think could be happy for us may surprise us

If they have the capacity, then we probably do too

Say thank you for being happy for me

Thank you for restoring my faith in human capacity for sympathetic joy

Thank you, universe, for sending me this person and their sympathetic joy today

It may be difficult but removing the negativity and at least moving to neutrality is the first step to sympathetic joy

Now imagine being happy for them

You may be feeling a bit warmer towards them

How would you react to their success and happiness?

Can you reflect their joy?

How does it feel to be generous in spirit?
And they modeled it for you in your mind's eye
For this one second, can you be united in joy with them?
Join in their joy
Say thank you for sharing your happiness
Thank you for being happy
For giving you a chance to experience the opening of your heart
Softening of your spine
To change our minds
Thank you, universe, for giving this opportunity to experience joy through and for others
And creating a positive cycle of sympathetic joy
Because we are all one
The pauper and the prince
The oppressor and the oppressed
The saint and the scoundrel
Keep that moment of connection with others, with the universe in your heart
Remind yourself of this feeling when you cultivate sympathetic joy
Very deliberately, very intentionally, very mindfully
Thank you for joining me in this practice
Let's close with three breaths
Breathe in ...
Breathe out ...
This universe can be very expansive
It is expansive
We can be expansive
By opening our circles of care, concern, and morality, and joy
Breathe in ...
Breathe out ...
Smile
Breathe in ...
Breathe out ...
Stay as long as you wish in this moment
When you are ready, gently open your eyes

******

Daily Activity: Your Identity Tree – Part 3

Begin with a brief grounding meditative breath. Sit or stand comfortably anchored by your beautiful feet to the ground. Close your eyes if you haven't already done so. Take three deep breaths to clear your mind.

Inhale ... Exhale ...

Inhale ... Exhale ...

Inhale ... Exhale ...

Repeat after me:

I promise to engage in this contemplative practice fully, mindfully, thoughtfully, heartfully, and non-judgmentally. I believe that we all can learn and grow. Our identities can shift shape with time and knowledge. I will be open to such change.

Now open your eyes. Then pick up your tree drawing and add the compost on the ground away from the tree.

The compost

- List things, organizations, beliefs, or people you have left behind because they did not serve you.
- List things, organizations, beliefs, or people that do not serve you well and you wish to leave.
- Place them next to your ground.
- How does getting rid of these things or beliefs or relationships shape or change your identity?

Journal Prompt

What is in your compost? What resentments do you hold due to your identities? How do you bring sympathetic joy to those who have hurt you, victimized you or made you feel weak?

Day 25

Guilt to Gratitude and Generosity

In this meditation, musing, contemplation, we are going to be think about survivor's guilt. During the pandemic every day I wake up feeling relieved that I am not sick. That my family members are safe. With the relief, there is also guilt. Especially as someone whose home is New York. I could not escape my surroundings. Similarly, if we are privileged or fortunate in any way and we are thoughtful and empathetic, it is not uncommon to feel the guilt. But guilt is somewhat useless unless we convert it into compost and feed our tree's health and vibrancy. So this meditation practice is going to be reframing guilt into gratitude.

Take a comfortable position

Close your eyes if you like

Plant your feet

Connect to Mother Earth

And begin this practice with three deep, delicious breaths

Inhale ...

Exhale ...
Inhale ...
Exhale ...
Inhale ...
Exhale ...
Now, focus on the guilt
And think about where the guilt comes from
What does the guilt feel like?
Where does it sit in your body?
Do you feel you are underserving or unworthy?
Does it sit in your stomach?
Does it pour through eyes?
Does it give you a panic attack?
What does guilt do?
Does it make you depressed?
Think of the souls that have departed
Send love to their families
Send healing thoughts to their families that have been left behind
Say I love you
I send you healing thoughts and love
I cannot even imagine that kind of loss
And I hope you get some peace and comfort in these times of loss
I send you, through me, the love of the universe
Maybe you have a job, while others you know have lost theirs
Maybe that is the source of your guilt
But is that guilt a useful emotion?
Is guilt helping you?
Pay attention to that guilt
Be kind to yourself
And ask
"How does that guilt help you, your family or people that you serve, or anyone?"
Even those who have lost their jobs
Can we reframe that guilt into generosity?
Can you extend your kindness, your generosity to those whose losses make you feel guilty?
Send them your love
Send them your support as a member of the community
Maybe you feel guilty about all the essential workers that keep our lives going
The first responders, the transit workers, the grocery store stockers, the delivery people, the postal workers, the firemen, the police, the EMS workers, all of those who keep our world moving and our basic services intact

If you are feeling guilty about them working and risking their health for you
And you are inside safe
While they are risking their health for us
You can convert this guilt into gratitude
This guilt into generosity
Send them your love, your gratitude
Say thank you for keeping my city going, for keeping my family fed
For keeping my community safe
Make a vow to yourself
That you will engage in an action of generosity
Maybe you are not making enough money to donate
Maybe it is time to donate
Maybe you will remember to be kind and say thank you to them when you see them on the street
In the store
Convert guilt into gratitude
Convert guilt into generosity
Grief and guilt ask the same question in mirroring ways
Grief asks why me
Guilt asks why not me
Both involve a puzzlement
Because we like things to be logical
That calms us
That the world is controllable
We can actually explain the connection between A and B and how things work
When things happen inexplicably, that means the world is out of whack
We can't explain why some good things happen to us randomly or some bad things happen to us randomly
And in this moment of crisis and pandemic, these things happen in a condensed and heightened way
So be intentional about accepting the randomness
Despite everything we do and try
We have social distanced
We have masked
We have gloved
We have isolated ourselves
Some of us haven't received a hug in a long time
Some of us haven't seen anyone else in a long time
Despite all this, there is a randomness
Yes, we can explain things through structural inequalities
But still there is a randomness
The hardest thing is to accept the randomness because we lose control

As much as money should protect us, and it does

Sometimes even that privilege doesn't protect us or our lives

So, the guilt and the grief, they are equally random

Except that we cannot control everything that happens on the planet and the universe

Even if there are rational mechanisms that can explain things over time

We cannot control them

Or even explain them in a shorter time frame, when crisis attacks

Accept the randomness

Tell yourself that you are going to do your best to protect yourself and others

But you are going to get comfortable with the uncertainty of randomness

You can do a lot, but you cannot control everything

And that is okay

Why is it okay?

You should be able to control and make life better for everyone

Yes, we must try

But there is a margin and in that margin of uncertainty, trying raises stress

Stress raises our recklessness and carelessness

Stress lowers our immunity

It raises our inability to self-regulate

In that margin between what we have control over and what we don't, accepting the randomness and the uncertainty is counter-intuitively more productive

That keeps us healthy, sane, grounded, generous, less anxious and stronger

Take three deep breaths again

Inhale …

Exhale gratitude

Inhale your anxiety and guilt

Why not me?

Exhale generosity, kindness, love

Inhale …

Exhale …

Make a commitment

I will not forget those who risked their lives for me during the pandemic

I will remember and honor their work after it is all done

I will remember and honor their work for the community

I will remember and honor those who passed and their families that grieved

I will remember to always be generous and kind

I will remember to always convert my guilt into gratitude and generosity

Take a deep breath

Say thank you to the universe
Commit to generosity
You really have the power to reframe your perspective
Guilt is not really useful
Instead convert it to gratitude and generosity
It will empower you and help other people
Sending you all love
Thank you for joining this practice

******

Daily Activity: Integrate Your Identity Tree Exercise

Now look at the whole tree, make any corrections until you feel comfortable with on your identity tree.

Journal Prompt

What parts of your identity and life make you feel guilty? How do you atone for them? How can you convert your guilt into gratitude and generosity?

Day 26

Gift Culture Meditation

In this meditation, we are focusing on the idea that we are all interconnected.

That we can move from merely transactional and financial and focus on connections, relationships, generosity, and trust even with strangers that we may not know.

In this imagined economy or culture, the most powerful is the most generous.
We begin with an anchoring breath
Breathe in ...
Breathe out ...
Breathe in ...
Breathe out ...
Think about a time that you gave something to someone
Or helped someone with no expectation of return
How did that feel?
What triggered that generosity?
When you feel like giving something to someone or helping someone
Do you think many times before making a decision?
Does emotion or thought move you more to gifting?

I find that when my spirit moves me to give, doing it right away helps me
Otherwise, I find that I start to think, rationalize, and I end up not giving
Unlike impulse purchases, I impulse gift or donate
Breathe in ...
Breathe out ...
Breathe in ...
Breathe out ...
Breathe in ...
Breathe out ...
Think of a time when someone gave you a gift
A gift of an idea, an introduction, or a check when you needed it most
How did it feel to be the recipient?
What do you think they received in return?
Do you ever gift it forward?
Perhaps you were a student who was helped by someone in your university
And you never forgot and now volunteer your time
Gift culture is moving beyond reciprocity of give and take in a shorter
time frame
It is expanding our circle of moral concern and care
It is expanding our time horizon to seven generations
It is understanding that we are all one
Like the indigenous who protected our Mother Earth for seven generations
What do you gift the world?
What is your legacy?
Thank you for joining this practice
We close with three deep breaths
Breathe in ...
Breathe out
Breathe in ...
Breathe out ...
Breathe in ...
Breathe out ...
Open your eyes when you are ready

******

Daily Activity: Leadership Philosophy

If being a leader is your gift to the world, what would your philosophy be?

- Step 1: Set a timer for 20 minutes
- Step 2: Write a free-flowing, stream of consciousness statement of your leadership philosophy.
- Step 3: Complete and save or put it away until tomorrow.

Journal Prompt

When was the last time you gave a gift to someone you loved? Or someone you didn't even know? How does gift-giving make you feel?

Day 27

Ideal Self in the Universe

In this meditation, we are going to try and develop a picture of what your ideal or highest universal self.

As usual, we begin with the breath and commit to kindness and compassion to self. It is easy to focus on the gaps between who we wish to be and how we show up right now, but we want to focus on our highest aspirations for ourselves.

Take three deep grounding breaths
Breathe in ...
Breathe out ...
Breathe in ...
Breathe out ...
Breathe in ...
Breathe out ...
Now connect to your entire body
Ground in your body
Feel who you are
From head to toe
Feel the oxygen pulsing through your body
Its every cell
Feel being open, confident, kind, and joyful
Open to possibilities, opportunities, responsibilities
Bring to mind your immediate circle of relationships
Partner, child, parent, friends, and family
How do you show up with them?
What is your ideal self in this circle of intimates?
This is your relational ideal self
Breathe in ...
Breathe out ...
Breathe in ...
Breathe out ...
What kind of partner or parent or child do you want to be?
Sibling and friend
How do you want to be seen by this group of people?
Can you see them being proud of you?
Can you see what their needs are?

Can you see how they need you to show up?
What would it take for you to show up that way?
Breathe in ...
Breathe out ...
Breathe in ...
Breathe out ...
Breathe in ...
Breathe out ...
Now expand your circle beyond your immediate friends and family
Consider other groups you belong to
Or organizations you are part of
Or maybe your work
Who are these people?
What are the value alignments between you and them?
Do they give you purpose?
Do they give you energy? Affirmation for your personhood?
What kind of commitment do you feel towards them?
How do you show up for these groups and people?
How do they need you to show up?
What would it take for you to show up in that way?
Breathe in ...
Breathe out ...
Breathe in ...
Breathe out ...
Breathe in ...
Breathe out ...
How do you show up for your community?
How do they need you to show up?
How would you like to show up and be seen by them?
Breathe in ...
Breathe out ...
Breathe in ...
Breathe out ...
Breathe out ...
You are comfortable, grounded, safe
Safe enough to be open and curious
You are calm and relaxed
Your body is relaxed
Your mind is alert
There is no stress
All that is important to be my best self
To be happy
To be joyful
To be curious

To be playful
To be passionate
To be faithful
To your partner, your faith, your community
To be engaged
To be held in a circle of love
By your family
By your friends
To be held in esteem
By your colleagues
By your peers
Savor that moment
Say thank you
Tell them you will see them in ten years
Take a deep breath
Breathe in ...
Breathe out ...
Breathe in ...
Breathe out ...
Now imagine you in resonance with the universe
All the beings in the universe
If you are connected and one with everything in the universe
How would you show up?
How does the universe need you to show up?
What would it take for you to show up that way?
Hold this image in your mind
For it is your most expansive self
We may shrink from it
We may forget it
But this connection has the power to nurture us immeasurably
Keep it close to your heart
Where you can come to it when you need it
Take a deep breath
Breathe in ...
Breathe out ...
Thank you for joining in this practice
Open your eyes gently when you are comfortable

******

Daily Activity: What Are Your Mental Models?

Respond to the following statements using a five-point scale (1 being strongly disagree to 5 being strongly agree).

1   I believe that there is a larger meaning to life.
2   It is important for me to give something back to my community.
3   I have had moments of great joy in which I suddenly had a clear, deep feeling of oneness with all that exists.
4   Sometimes I feel so connected to nature that everything seems to be part of one organism.
5   Life is most worthwhile when it is lived in service to an important cause.
6   I feel my life is best served when I serve my immediate community.
7   I am easily and deeply touched when I see human misery and suffering.
8   I think about how my decisions will influence the long-term consequences.
9   Humans are mutually responsible to and for one another.
10 I feel connected to the organization/s to which I belong.
11 I think each city/region/country must take care of itself first.
12 Human beings are responsible for protecting the planet and all that inhabit the Earth.
13 There is a plane of consciousness that binds all sentient beings.
14 I feel that I have a calling to fulfill in life.
15 I am concerned about those who will come after me in life.
16 All life is interconnected.
17 I believe that on some level my life is intimately tied to all of humankind.
18 I love the blooming of flowers in the spring as much as seeing an old friend again.
19 I think I need to take care of the people around me.
20 I believe that my life is intimately tied to all of universe.

Journal Prompt

What is the identity orientation most comfortable for you – personal, relational, communal, or universal? Depending on where your comfort zone is, how do you manage your boundaries between your individual, interpersonal/relational, tribal/communal, and universal/expansive identities? How do they conflict with each other? How do you resolve the conflict?

Day 28

Universal Loving Kindness Meditation

Settle into the awareness of the body and the breath
  Breathe in …
  Breathe out …
  Breathe in …
  Breathe out …
  After you have connected with the breath
  Feel your body

Notice what is there
Connect your breath to your body
Breathe in ...
Breathe out ...
Be open to whatever you can experience in the moment, in the body
Feel the breath moving through your heart
We first begin with loving kindness towards ourselves
Allowing our heart to open with tenderness
Remember your basic goodness
Maybe you want to remember a time when you were kind or generous
And your natural desire to be happy and not to suffer
If you are finding it difficult to acknowledge your own goodness
Look at yourself through the eyes of someone who loves you
What does that person love about you?
Or you may recall the unconditional love that you felt from your pet
And some of us find it hard
If you find it even harder
Use your imagination and picture yourself as a young child
Feel the tender feelings that you would feel towards this young child
As you experience this love
Notice how you feel in your body
Maybe you feel warm or some heat or a smile
Or a sense of expansiveness
This is loving kindness
A natural feeling that is accessible to all of us
Rest for a few moments with this feeling
Of open and unconditional love for yourself
Bask in that loving kindness towards yourself
Breathe in ...
Breathe out ...
What does it feel like to feel the acceptance?
Now, make a wish for yourself
May I be happy
May I be peaceful
May I be held in loving kindness
May I feel filled with loving kindness
May I feel centered and calm
May I feel connected and calm
May I know the natural joy of being alive
May I be safe
May I be peaceful and at ease
If there are feelings of warmth or friendliness or love in your body or mind
Connect to them
Allow them to grow

Direct the loving kindness to yourself
Then bring to mind a friend or someone in your life who has deeply cared for you
And send your loving kindness to them
May you be happy
May you be well
May you be safe and peaceful
May you be the recipient of loving kindness
May you be filled with loving kindness
Sink into the intention and the heartfelt feeling you have for this person
They have done so much for you
You feel love for them
Affection, warmth, acceptance
Feel the feelings and send them your good intentions
Connect the feelings to the phrases
As you continue, open the circle to someone that is neutral
You may see them regularly but not know them well
Could be a neighbor
Someone at the store
Somebody that you know of, but you don't know well
Bring this person to your mind now
And use the same phrases
May you be happy
May you be well
May you be safe
May you be peaceful and at ease
May you receive loving kindness
May you be filled with loving kindness
Sometimes during this meditation you might even feel the opposite feelings
Anger, grief, or sadness
That is a good sign that your heart is softening
Accept that with whatever patience and kindness you can muster for the same feelings
Instead, direct loving kindness towards them
Now bring to mind someone with whom you have had a difficult relationship
Perhaps it is someone you find difficult to like or feel compassion
This is the time to remind yourself that this person is a whole being
They also need loving kindness
As someone who may feel pain and anxiety
As someone who may suffer
As someone as human as you are
See if it is possible to extend the words of loving kindness to these people or this person
May you be safe

May you be happy
May you feel my love now
May you feel loving kindness
May you be filled with loving kindness
Now allow your awareness to spread in all directions
Imagine that you are standing in a vast space
That you can connect to everyone and everything
Yourself, people whom you love
People to whom you feel neutral
People to whom you feel negative
All human beings, all animals
The rich tapestry of the universe
With all the prospects for joy and sorrow
War and peace
Hunger, abundance
Love, joy, anger, everything that composes your mind and the world
And now, send the loving kindness to everyone and everything
May you be safe
May you be happy
May you feel loving kindness
May you be filled with loving kindness
May all beings be filled with loving kindness
May all beings be happy
May all beings be awakened and free
May all beings be safe
Now, come back to yourself and see how you feel
If you feel the love and the warmth in your body
In your heart, in your face
Sometimes it is even in the toes
Bask in the energy of loving kindness that you have generated
And the people that practice this all over the world have generated
Connect back to your breath
Breathe in ...
Breathe out ...
Breathe in ...
Breathe out ...
Enjoy the feeling
Breathe in ...
Breathe out ...
Take this moment to connect with yourself and with the universe
With love and kindness and compassion
And gently open your eyes

******

Daily Activity: Finalize Your Leadership Philosophy

What is your leadership philosophy? How do you want to show up as a leader?

Journal Prompt

Who are you?

Note

1 Denborough, D. (2014). *Retelling the Stories of Our Lives: Everyday Narrative Therapy to Draw Inspiration and Transform Experience.* New York, NY: W. W. Norton & Company.

Epilogue
Integrating and Renewing

If you got to Day 28, you are committed, tenacious, and dedicated. I have no doubt that you will be able to continue this further on your own, practice mediation and other mindfulness practice, and move forward mindfully, intentionally, and grounded in expansive, transcendental, and interdependence centric mental models. In this chapter, we begin with renewal and commitment mediation practice, wrap-up the journey for now, and develop personal plans for continuing the practice and planning for renewal.

Renewed Commitment Meditation

Close your eyes
   Plant your feet
   I always like connecting our feet to Mother Earth
   We are always busy and flying
   Walking to meetings, running to class
   This is something you can do anywhere even for thirty seconds to reground yourself
   You are waiting for something, a meeting, to pick up coffee
   You can connect to the earth and ground yourself
   Let's do three deep breaths
   To set an intention for this upcoming period
   To stay grounded
   To connect our bodies to our thoughts
   To our breath
   To our emotions
   To our hopes and dreams
   Inhale ...
   Exhale ...
   Inhale ...
   Exhale ...
   Inhale ...

Exhale …
Pay attention to your left foot
How does it feel to be connected to the ground?
How does your foot feel?
Then direct your attention to your left ankle
Send an imaginary light to your body
To your left ankle
We are almost always disconnected from our bodies
Most of our jobs require us to be in our heads
Some of us may be lucky enough to be artists, chefs, people that use their
hands
But most of us don't
It is nice to connect to our bodies
From your ankle to your calf
Pay attention
Maybe you need to stretch, and you can feel it
Maybe you went for a run this morning and you can feel it
Then move to your knee
Your kneecap
Sometimes we take our bodies for granted
Most times, actually
It is a nice way to stay grounded and anchored
But also, just pay attention to your body
Be grateful
Now move up to your left thigh
And then think of you doing a mind massage
You can also use your fingers to give yourself a little massage
Move to your left hip
Think of a gingerbread man drawing we did as a child
Go up to your waist
Your left shoulder
Pay attention to your shoulder
How does it feel?
Pay attention to your left arm
All the way to your fingers
Think of directing energy, gratitude, light, attention to your own body
Sometimes you feel a tingle
Sometimes cold
Sometimes warm
Your skin may feel different when you pay attention
Now let's begin the process with your right foot
See how your toes feel
See if you can spot a difference between your right and left foot
Our body operates differently in both sides

We don't notice most of the time
But our body knows
So, it automatically favors one side or the other
Right foot to your right ankle
We move up
Right calf
Your right knee
Your thigh
Your hips
Your entire pelvic area where you are seated
It holds all your organs
Pay attention to it
Move up to your waist, shoulder, arm
Again, think about whether your right and left sides feel different
Our dominant hand may feel different from our non-dominant hand
Pay attention, move from your right shoulder to your right hand
Now direct your attention back to your pelvis
See how you feel
Do you feel safely held?
Grounded?
Connected?
We pay attention to our biceps and triceps and forget our core
That which grounds us
Our pelvic area
Your feet hold the weight of your body
Your pelvic area holds all your organs
Direct your attention to your spinal cord
It is a good time to sit up tall
Imagine a silver thread holding you up
Some people prefer a shaft of light
Visual metaphors are powerful
They can help us pay attention
And sit all
Pay attention to your vertebrate
Direct your attention to your neck
Is your neck loose?
Tight?
Is there any anxiety?
Sometimes this whole practice can be discomforting
Part of the mindfulness goal is to stay with the discomfort
Not to suffer
But to observe
Your neck
Your head

Pay attention to your face
How does it feel?
Your skin?
Are you are tight in the face?
Sometimes we don't notice our face is tight
If it is tight, loosen your face muscles, your jaw
There is a strong body and mind connection
If you are tense in your body, it is difficult to be open in the mind
Set an intention to practice everyday
This is a sacred space
That which we hold sacred
In which we hold each other sacred
Be responsible for each other's growth and learning
Let's close with three more breaths
Inhale ...
Exhale ...
Inhale ...
Exhale ...
Inhale ...
Exhale ...
Thank you for joining this practice
Open your eyes gently when you are comfortable

******

Integrative Activity: Identities and Mental Models

- Step 1: Collect all the work you have done so far, including all the identity pieces, journals and your identity tree.
- Step 2: What do you want to let go? What do you want to keep?
- Step 3: Who are you? What are your mental models? How do you want to show up in the world?

Final Journal Prompt

How was your overall experience? How do you want to continue this practice?

******

I thank you for joining me on this journey and trusting me with your core self. I wish to close with this prayer for me, for you, and for the universe at large.

Bhumi-Mangalam, Udaka-Mangalam, Agni-Mangalam, Vayu-Mangalam, Gagana-Mangalam, Surya-Mangalam, Chandra-Mangalam, Jagat-Mangalam, Jiva-Mangalam, Deha-Mangalam, Mano-Mangalam, Atma-Mangalam, Sarva-Mangalam-Bhavatu-Bhavatu-Bhavatu ...

May there be peace on earth, water, fire, sky, air, the sun, the moon, and the planet, in all living beings, in body, mind, heart and soul. May that peace be everywhere and in everyone.

Index